Veni

Beryl De Zoete, Mary Sturge Gretton

Alpha Editions

This edition published in 2024

ISBN : 9789362927033

Design and Setting By
Alpha Editions
www.alphaedis.com
Email - info@alphaedis.com

Contents

Contents

Chapter One
INTRODUCTORY

"VENICE herself is poetry, and creates a poet out of the dullest clay." It was a poet who spoke, and his clay was instinct with the breath of genius. But it is true that Venice lends wings to duller clay; it has been her fate to make poets of many who were not so before—a responsibility that entails loss on her as well as gain.

She has lived—she has loved and suffered and created; and the echoes of her creation are with us still; the pulse of the life which once she knew continues to throb behind the loud and insistent present. The story of Venice has been often written; the Bride of the Adriatic, in her decay as in her youthful and her mature beauty, has been the beloved of many men. "Wo betide the wretch," cries Landor through the mouth of Machiavelli, "who desecrates and humiliates her; she may fall, but she shall rise again." Venice even then had passed her zenith; the path she had entered, though blazing with a glory which had not attended on her dawn of life, was yet a path of decline, the resplendent, dazzling path of the setting sun. And now a second Attilla, as Napoleon vaunted himself, has descended upon her. She has been desecrated, but she has never been dethroned. She could not, if she would, take the ring off her finger. No hand of man, however potent, can destroy that once consummated union, however the stranger and her traitor sons may abase her from within.

It is to her own domain, embraced by her mutable yet eternally faithful ocean-lover, that we must still go to see the relics of her pomp. The old sternness has passed from her face, that compelling sovereignty which gave her rank among the greatest potentates of the Middle Age; her features, portrayed by these latter days, are mellowed; a veil of golden haze softens the bold outlines of that imperious countenance. We are sometimes tempted to forget that the cup held by the enchanter, Venice, was filled once with no dream-inducing liquor, but with a strong potion to fire the nerves of heroes. Viewing Venice in her greater days, it is impossible to make that separation between the artist and the man of action so deadly to action and to art. The portraits of the Venetian masters, supreme among the portraits of the world, could only have been produced by men who beyond the divine perception of form and colour were endowed with a profound understanding and divination of human character. The pictures of Gentile Bellini, of Carpaccio, of Mansueti, are a gallery of portraits of stern, strong, capable, self-confident men; and Giovanni Bellini, who turned from secular themes to concentrate his energy on the portrayal of the Madonna and Child, endowed her with a strength and solemn pathos which only Giotto could rival, combined with a luminous richness of colour in which perhaps he has no rival at all.

No mystics have sprung from Venice. Her sons have been artists of life, not dreamers, though the sea, that great weaver of dreams, has been ever around them. Or rather it is truer to say that the dreamers of Venice have also been men of action; strong, capable and intensely practical. They have not turned their back on the practice of life; they have loved it in all its forms. Even when they speak through the medium of allegory, of symbols, the art of Carpaccio and of Tintoretto is a supreme record of the interests of the greatest Venetians in the actions of everything living in this wonderful world, and in particular—they are not ashamed to own it—in their supremely wonderful city of Venice. There are dreamers among those crowds of Carpaccio, of Gentile Bellini; but their hands can grasp the weapons and the tools of earth; their heads and hearts can wrestle with the problems and passions of earth. Compare them with the dreamers of Perugino's school: you feel at once that a gulf lies between them; the fabric of their dream is of another substance. The great Venetians are giants; like the sea's, their embrace is vast and powerful, endowed also with the gentleness of strength. The history of Venetian greatness in art, in politics, in theology, is the history of men who have accepted life and strenuously devoted themselves to mastering its laws. They were not iconoclasts, because they were not idolaters: the faculties of temperance and restraint are apparent in their very enthusiasms. Venice did not fall because she loved life too well, but because she had lost the secret of living. Pride became to her more beautiful than truth, and finally more worshipful than beauty.

Much has, with truth, been said about the destruction of Venice. Even in those who have not known her as she was, who in presence of her wealth remaining are unconscious of the greatness of her loss, there constantly stirs indignant sorrow at the childish wantonness of her inhabitants, which loves to destroy and asks only a newer and brighter plaything. But much persists that is indestructible; and though Venice has become a spectacle for strangers, for those who are her lovers the old spirit lingers still near the form it once so gloriously inhabited, wakened into being, perchance, by a motion, an echo, a light upon the waters, and once wakened never again lost or out of mind. Does not the silent swiftness of the Ten still haunt the sandolo of the water police, as it steals in the darkness with unlighted lamp under the shadow of larger craft moored beside the fondamenta, visible only when it crosses the path of a light from house or garden? It is in her water that Venice eternally lives; it is thus that we think always of her image—elusive, unfathomable, though plumbed so often by no novice hand. It is the wonder of Venice within her waters which justifies the renewal of the old attempt to reconstruct certain aspects of a career which has been a challenge to the world, a mystery on which it has never grown weary of speculating. And as the light falling from a new angle on familiar features may reveal some grace hidden heretofore in shadow or unobserved, so, perchance, the vision of Venice may be renewed or kindled through the medium of a new personality.

Venice is inexhaustible, and it is from her waters that her mine of wealth is drawn. They give her wings; without them she would be fettered like other cities of the land. But Venice with her waters is never dead. The sun may fall with cruel blankness on calle, piazza and fondamenta, but nothing can kill the water; it is always mobile, always alive. Imagine the thoroughfare of an inland city on such a day as is portrayed in Manet's *Grand Canal de Venise*; heart and eye would curse the sunshine. But in the luminous truth of Manet's picture, as in Venice herself, the heat quivers and lives. Above ground, blue sky beating down on blue canal, on the sleepy midday motion of the gondolas, on the brilliant blue of the striped gondola posts, which appear to stagger into the water; and under the surface, the secret of Venice, the region where reflections lurk, where the long wavering lines are carried on in the deep, cool, liquid life below. When Venice is weary, what should she do but dive into the water as all her children do? If we look down, when we can look up no longer, still she is there; a city more shadowy but not less real, her elements all dissolved that at our pleasure we may build them again;

And so not build at all,

And therefore build for ever.

VIEW FROM THE GALLERY OF SAN MARCO.

And if in the middle day we realise this priceless dowry of Venice, it is in the twilight of morning or evening that her treasury is unlocked and she invites us to enter. Turner's *Approach to Venice* is a vision, a dream, but not more divinely lovely than the reality of Venice in these hours, even as she appears to duller eyes. Pass down the Grand Canal in the twilight of an August evening, the full moon already high and pouring a lustre from her pale green halo on the broad sweeping path of the Canal. The noble curves of the houses to west and south shut out the light; day is past, the reign of night has begun. Then cross to the Zattere: you pass into another day. A full tide flows from east to west, blue and swelling like the sea, dyed in the west a shining orange Where the Euganean hills rise in clear soft outline against the afterglow, while to the east the moon has laid her silver bridle upon the dim waters. Cross to the Giudecca and pass along the narrow, crowded quay into the old palace, which in that deserted corner shows one dim lamp to the canal. The great hall opens at the further end on a bowery garden where a fountain drips in the darkness and the cicalas begin their piping. Mount the winding stair, past the kitchen and the great key-shaped reception room, and look out over the city—across the whole sweep of the magnificent Giudecca Canal and the basin of San Marco. The orange glow is fading and the Euganean hills are dying into the night, while near at hand one great golden star is setting behind the Church of the Redentore, and the moon shines with full brilliance upon the swaying waters, upon the Ducal Palace and the churches of the Zattere, with the Salute as their chief. The night of Venice has begun; she has put on her jewels and is blazing with light. At the back of the house, where the lagoons lie in the shimmering moonlight, is a silent waste of waters under the stars, broken only by the lights of the islands. This also is Venice, this mystery of moonlit water no less than the radiance of the city. And it is possible to come still nearer to the lagoon. Passing along a dark rio little changed from the past, we may cross a bridge into one of the wonderful gardens for which the Giudecca is famous. The families of the Silvi, Barbolini and Istoili, banished in the ninth century for stirring up tumult in the Republic, when at last they were recalled by intercession of Emperor Ludovico, inhabited this island of Spinalunga or Giudecca and laid out gardens there. This one seems made for the night. The moonlight streams through the vine pergolas which cross it in every direction, lights the broad leaves of the banana tree and the dome of the Salute behind the dark cypress-spire, and stars the grass with shining petals. The night is full of the scent of haystacks built along the edge of the lagoon, beside the green terrace which runs the length of the water-wall. Then, as darkness deepens, we leave to the cicalas their moonlit paradise, and glide once more into the Grand Canal. It is at this hour, more than at any other, that, sweeping round the curves of that marvellous waterway, it possesses us as an idea, a presence that is not to be put by, so compelling, so vitally creative, is its beauty. Truly Venice is poetry, and would create a poet out of the dullest clay.

Every one will remember that a few years ago an enterprising man of business attempted with sublime self-confidence to transfer Venice to London, to enclose her within the walls of a great exhibition. Many of us delighted in the miniature market of Rialto, in gliding through the narrow waterways, in the cry of the gondoliers, and the sound of violin and song across the water. But one gift in the portion of Venice was forgotten, a gift which she shares indeed with other cities, but which she alone can put out to interest and increase a thousandfold. The sky is the roof of all the world, but Venice alone is paved with sky; and the streets of Venice with no sky above them are like the wings of the butterfly without the sun. Tintoret and Turner saw Venice as the offspring of sky and water: that is the spirit in which they have portrayed her; that is the essence of her life. It has penetrated everything she has created of enduring beauty. Go into San Marco and look down at what your feet are treading. Venice, whose streets are paved with sky, must in her church also have sky beneath her feet. It is impossible to imagine a more wonderful pavement than the undulating marbles of San Marco; its rich and varied colours bound together with the rarest inspiration; orient gems captured and imprisoned and constantly lit with new and vivid beauty from the domes above. The floor of San Marco is one of the glories of Venice—of the world; and it is surely peculiarly expressive of the inspiration which worked in Venice in the days of her creative life. San Marco, indeed, in its superb and dazzling harmonies of colour, is almost the only living representative of the Venice of pomegranate and gold which created the Cà d'Oro, of the City of Carpaccio and Gentile Bellini, whose cornice-mouldings were interwoven with glittering golden thread, while every side canal gave back a glow of colour from richly-tinted walls. The banners of the Lion in the Piazza no longer wave in solemn splendour of crimson and gold above a pavement of pale luminous red; in their place the tricolour of Italy flaunts over colourless uniformity. The gold is fading from the Palace of the Doges, and only in a few rare nooks, such as the Scuola of the Shoemakers in the Campo San Tomà, do we find the original colours of an old relief linger in delicate gradation over window or door.

Day after day some intimate treasure is torn from the heart of Venice. Since Ruskin wrote, one leaf after another has been cut from the Missal which "once lay open upon the waves, miraculous, like St. Cuthbert's book, a golden legend on countless leaves." Those leaves are numbered now. Year by year some familiar object disappears from bridge or doorway, to be labelled and hoarded in a distant museum among aliens and exiles like itself. And here, in Venice itself, a sentiment of distress, the *fastidio* of the Italians, comes over us as we ponder upon the sculptured relics in the cortile of the Museo Civico. What meaning have they here? It is atmosphere that they need—the natural surroundings that would explain and vivify their forms. Many also of the Venetian churches are despoiled, and their paintings hung side by side with alien subjects in a light they were never intended to bear. The Austrian had less power to hurt Venice than she herself possesses. In those of her sons who understand her malady there flows an undercurrent of deep sadness, as if day by day they watched the ebbing of a life in which all their hope and all their love had root. They cannot sever themselves from Venice: they cannot save her. Venice pretending to share in the vulgar life of to-day, Venice recklessly discarding one glory after another for the poor exchange of coin, still has a power over us not wielded by the inland cities of Italy, happier in the untroubled beauty of their decay. For, as you are turning with sorrow from some fresh sign of pitiless destruction, of a sudden she will flash upon you a new facet of her magic stone, will draw you spell-bound to her waters and weave once more that diaphanous web of radiant mystery:

Za per dirtelo,—o Catina,

La campagna me consola;

Ma Venezia è la sola

Che me possa contentar.

Each of us, face to face with Venice, has a new question to ask of her, and, as he alone framed the question, the answer will be given to him alone. Every stone has not yielded up its secret: in some there may still be a mark yet unperceived beneath the dust. Here and there in her manuscript there may lurk between the lines a word for the skilled or the fortunate. Venice is not yet dumb: every day and every night the sun and moon and star make music in her that has not yet been heard: with patience and love we may redeem here and there a chord of those divine musicians, or at least a tone which shall make her harmony more full.

O Venezia benedetta,

No te vogio più lassar.

Chapter Two
PHANTOMS OF THE LAGOONS

WE have called them the phantoms of the lagoons, those islands that lie like shadows among the silver waters; for it is in this likeness that they appear to us of the city—strangely mirrored, remote, a group of clustering spirits, whose common halo is the sea. They are a choir of spirits, yet each has a mute music of its own, and accosting them one by one—slowly and in the silence entering into their life—we may come to know and love the several members of this company of the blest, till our senses grow alive to their harmony as they sing together, sometimes in the clear, cold light of the spreading dawn, sometimes in the evening twilight—when peak after peak is lit with the flame of sacrifice and, in the Titanic memory of the sunset cloud, the great fire lit on earth burns up with solemn flames into the sky.

All the languors, the fierce passions, of Venice, her vitality and her mysticism, are mirrored in the lagoons; there is no pulse of Venice that does not beat in them; in swift sequence, as in a lighter element, they reflect the phases of her being. And the islands of the lagoons are, as it were, the footsteps of young Venice. As she was passing into her kingdom, she set her feet here and there among the waters, and where she trod a life was born. Her roots are far back in the past, far up upon the mainland, where still remain some fragments of the giant growth, which, grafted in the lagoons, was to expand there into a new fulness of beauty and life. It is as if the genius that conceived Jesolo, Torcello, the Madonna of San Donato, had undergone a sea-change as it moved towards the Adriatic, as if some vision had passed before it and shaken it, as if the immutable had felt the first touch of mutability—had been endowed with a new sense born of the ebb and flow of ocean tides. In Malamocco she stepped too near the sea, and left behind the mystery of a city submerged; but no one can receive into his mind the peerless blue and green of the open water beyond the Lido, with the foam upon it, or the sound of its incessant sweep against the shore, without feeling that the spirit that had thus embraced the sea had received a new pulse into her being—a nerve of desire, of expansion, of motion, which her mountain infinitudes had not inspired. And with the new life came new dreams to Venice, dreams she was not slow to realise, and into them were woven materials for which we should seek in vain among the islands, except in so far as the reflex of her later activities fell also upon them. The Madonna of San Donato is the goddess of the lagoons; and if there are children of Venice who creep also for blessing and for protection to the borders of her dusky garment, they are but few. The mystic beauty of that Madonna was not the beauty that inspired Venice when she built upon the seas. The robe of her divinity was more akin to the dazzling incomparable blue of the bay that lies within the curve of the Schiavoni, as we may see it from the Palazzo Ducale on a morning of sunshine and east wind; that indomitable intensity of colour, unveiled, resplendent, filled to the brim with the whole radiance and strength and glory of the day—that is the girdle of Venice, the cup she drank of in her strength. But it is clear that she had bowed to a new dominion: with the ocean she wedded the world.

The lagoons are full of mysteries of light; they are a veritable treasure ground of illusion. They are not one expanse of water over which the light broods with equable influence; they form a region of various circles, as it were, of various degrees of remoteness or tangibility. Almost one feels that each circle must be inhabited by a spirit appropriate to itself, and that a common language could not be between them, so sharp are the limits set by the play of light. On an early autumn morning when the sky is clear and the sun streams full and level upon the clear blue expanse that separates Venice and Mestre, we seem to have a firm foothold on this dancing water. It is a substantial glory; but as our eye flits on from jewel to jewel in the clear blue paving, a sudden line is drawn beyond which it may not pass. The rich flood of vital colour has its bound, and beyond it lies a region bathed in light so intense that even colour is refined into a mystic whiteness—a mirror of crystal, devoid of substance, infinitely remote; and above it, suspended in that lucent unearthly atmosphere, hover the towers of Torcello and Burano, like a mirage of the desert, midway between the water and the sky. They hang there in completest isolation, yet with a precise definition, a startling clearness of contour. There is no vestige of other buildings or of the earth on which they stand, only the dome and campanile of Murano, the leaning spire of Burano and Mazzorbo's lightning-blasted tower, their reflections distinctly mirrored in a luminous medium, half mist, half water. There is an immense awe in the vision of these phantoms, caught up into a region where the happy radiant colour dares not play; and yet not veiled—clearer in what they choose to reveal than the near city strong and splendid in the unreserve of the young day, but so unearthly, so magical, that our morning spirits scarcely dare accost them. What boat shall navigate that shining nothingness that divides them from our brave and brilliant water?

Venice, indeed, at times falls under the phantom spell. In those mornings of late autumn when the duel between the sun and the scirocco seems as if it could not end till day is done and night calls up her reinforcements of mist, Venice is herself the ghost, her goblet brimming with a liquor that seems the drink of death, a perilous, grey, steely vapour. One only of her islands looms out of the enfolding, foggy blanket: it is San Michele, the island of the dead. On such a morning we may visit this abode of shadows, not at this hour more strange, more ghostly, than the city. To-day a veil is hung upon the hard, bare outline of its boundary wall, which in sunny weather is a glaring eye-sore as you travel towards Murano over the lagoon. Here, in the cloisters where once Fra Mauro dreamed and studied his famous Mappamondo, there is nothing to terrify the spirit on this morning of the mist. The black and tinsel drapings, the strange, unprofitable records of devotion and bereavement, the panoply of death—all these are veiled, and only the wild grasses glisten with their dewdrops on the graves of the very poor, or autumn leaves and flowers gleam from less humble graves, while the cypresses raise their solemn spires into the faintly dawning blue. But the cemetery island of San Michele together with the islands of the Giudecca and San Giorgio Maggiore, of San Pietro di Castello and Sant' Elena, with many lesser islands close to Venice, have become absorbed for us in the life of the city itself. Their bells and hers sound together; we see them as one with her, and from them look out to the wider lagoon, where the remoter islands, the true phantoms, wander. Many of those near to Venice have had their vicissitudes, their sometime glorious past, their pomp and solemn festival. But, bit by bit, it has been stolen from them, and the treasures which once they stored have been destroyed or gathered into the city. Now they serve only as shelters for those whose life is done—as places of repose for the dead or for the sick in mind and body. One only has passed from humble service into a fuller and happier present. San Lazzaro, once the shelter of lepers from the East, has become under the

Armenian Benedictines a haunt of active, cultured life. It has a living industry, printing the ancient trade of Venice, and is in daily commerce with the East.

SANTA MARIA DELLA SALUTE.

Torcello is a *città morta*, but scarcely a cemetery or a ruin. Relics of a past older than even Torcello has known are gathered into the humble urn of her museum; beside it stands abandoned, but not in ruins, the group of the cathedral buildings and the vast secular campanile; beyond this there is nothing but the soil—the golden gardens of vine and pomegranate, the fields of maize and artichokes between their narrow canals. The intervening period has entirely vanished; it is like a dream. The page of populous palatial Torcello has been blotted out as if it had had no existence. No vestige remains of the churches which in the old maps flourished along the chief canal, of the names which in the documents have no unsubstantial sound. None now can remember the time when the spoiler was busy among the ruined palaces; he too has passed into the shadows, and the very stones of Torcello are scattered far and wide. There is something mysterious in this complete wiping out of a page of history, so that not time only, but even the mourners of time have disappeared. There is something unique in the isolation of the cathedral and the campanile, rising thus out of the far past—this mighty masonry alone among the herbs of the field. Of her great history Torcello brings only the first page and the last, the duomo, the peasants' houses and the thatch shelters of their boats. Wandering along the grassy paths beside the vineyards, the pomegranates, the golden thorn bushes of Torcello, we seem in a sleepy pastoral land where the sun always shines. Torcello seems ripe, rich ground for a new life rather than the cemetery of an old; and we may feed the fancy as we will, for she does not refuse her doom; she has no hard contrasts of the old and new.

The few natives whom foreign gold supports upon this island of malaria, have their chief haunts in the cathedral campo, keeping guard over the treasures of the past. For here upon the campo stands the urn where Torcello keeps the ashes of her ancestors—strange relics of old Altinum, pathetic household gods, forks and spoons and safety-pins, keys and necklaces, lamps and broken plates and vases, chains and girdles and mighty bracelets, some of delicate and some of coarser make, with more ambitious works of mosaic and relief, Greek and Roman and Oriental. There is little in all; yet as we stand here in the museum, looking out through the sunny window on the hazy autumn gold of earth and the shimmering water beyond, this little speaks eloquently to the mind. Even to Torcello, the aged, these things are ancestral; their life was in the old Altinum when Torcello lay still undreamed-of in the womb of time. Climb the campanile, and you will wonder no more at the passing of the city at its feet; it is so mighty, so self-contained and now so voiceless with any tongue that earth can hear and understand; almost it seems as if that iron clapper, lying mute below the bell, were symbol of Torcello's farewell to the busy populous world that needs the call to prayer. The great tower is given up to mighty musings, and we upon its summit speculate no more on the forgotten Middle Age; we are content in the golden earth beneath our feet, in the soft dreamy azure of the encircling lagoon, where in the low tide the deep tracks wind and writhe like glistening water-snakes, or lie, like the faint transparent veining of a leaf, upon that smooth expanse of interchanging marsh and water, the uncertain dominion over which Torcello towers. For the campanile, in its vast simplicity of structure, its loneliness, its duration, is of kin with those great sentinels of the desert in which the Egyptians embodied their giant dreams of power. It is here that the soul of Torcello still abides, to dream out upon the mystery of day and night to the mountains and the city and the sea. And even if the sunlight is rich and jubilant in the yellow fields below, where the autumn has such fitting habitation, it spreads upon the waters a broad path of silver that gleams mysteriously like moonlight upon the distant spaces of the ocean shield, waking points of light out of the immense surrounding dimness. And it is most of all in the deep night that the gulf of the centuries may be bridged. The monotonous piping of the cicalas rises even to this height in the darkness, but no other sound is heard. It is a strangely moving, melancholy landscape, half hidden, half revealed, still holding in its patient, silent heart the tragic sorrows, the hopes and shattered longings, the courageous struggle of the past ages, the fierce cry of desolation, the flames of cities doomed to destruction in the darkness of night, and their ruins outspread beneath the unsparing sun. It has lain now so long deserted, a presence from which the stream of life has flowed away, carrying with it all the agitations of joy and sorrow, that among the fluctuating marshes the key for its deciphering has been lost.

As we have said, whole pages are torn from the history of Torcello. Fragments only remain. But here and there is a word or two that may be gathered into a sentence. If we approach the island from the east, by the waterway between Sant' Erasmo and Tre Porti instead of by the narrow channels of the inner lagoon, we may receive some impression of the relation it once bore to the mainland. We may see how Torcello stands as the entrance of the lagoon north of Venice, the last outpost of the mainland, the first-fruits of a new career—recognise that she was once through the Portus Torcellus in closest touch with the high seas. In the ninth century it was one Rustico of Torcello who combined with Buono of Malamocco to carry the bones of St. Mark from Alexandria to Venice. In 1 Torcello is specially mentioned by da Canale among the "Contrees, que armerent lor navie, et vindrent a lor signor Mesire Laurens Teuple (Lorenzo Tiepolo) li haut Dus de Venise, et a Madame la Duchoise" on the occasion of Tiepolo's election. Torcello contributed three galleys completely equipped for the Genoese war, and in 1463 sent one hundred crossbowmen in the service of the Republic against Trieste.

What is left of this city, which shared the early glory if not the later pomp of Venice? Where are her palaces, her gardens, her bridges, her waterways? Where are her piazzas and calles and fondamentas, her churches and rich convents? We pass their names in the old chronicles: Piazza del Duomo, Rio Campo di San Giovanni, Fondamenta dei Borgognoni, Calle Santa Margherita, Fondamenta Bobizo, Ponte di Chà Delfino, Ponte de Pino, and the rest. Many of these were of very old foundation: their stones and traces of their construction have been discovered from time to time under the mud of the canals. In the poor houses of the peasants traces still remain of original windows, cornices and pillars; the main canal is still spanned by the beautiful ruined bridge of the Diavolo. But for the rest the grass piazza with its little group of buildings, its museum flanked by the cathedral, is the sole echo, itself no more than an echo of the past.

When Altinum and her neighbouring cities roused themselves from the crushing desolation of conquest which had driven them forth to the remote borders of the mainland, they began to desire to live anew in the lagoons. There is no reason to question Dandolo's statement that Torcello and the group of surrounding islands, Burano, Mazzorbo, Constanziana, Amoriana and Ammiana, were named from the gates of Altinum—a pathetic attempt to perpetuate the ruined city. Nuovo Altino was indeed the name for Torcello, and when the terror of invasion had momentarily passed, the fugitives ventured back to the mainland, and brought down to the soft-soiled island the stones of their ancient city. Torcello was built from the stones of Altinum; her very stones were veterans, the stamp of old times was upon them, the stamp of thoughts that were often sealed for those men of a later day who built them anew into their temples. The steps up to the pulpit in the duomo are perhaps the most striking instance of this ingrafting of the old upon the new, the naïve earnestness, perhaps the urgent haste and need of builders who did not fear to set an old pagan relief to do service in this temple of their Christian God. There are various theories as to the meaning of the wonderful relief which forms the base of the pulpit stair, cut like its companion slabs to meet the requirements of the stair without regard to its individual existence. We cannot help pausing before it; for it is unique among the monuments of the estuary, so unique that it seems incredible it should have been the work of those late Greek artists who executed the wonderful beasts and birds of the sanctuary screen. On the right is a woman's figure, of Egyptian rather than Greek or Roman mould, standing with averted face and head resting on her arms, in melancholy thought. Beside her a man, like her resigned and meditative in attitude, but not yet with the resignation of despair, raises his left arm as if to ward off a blow. The blow is dealt left-handed by one who in his right hand holds a pair of scales and advances swiftly on winged wheels. He, again, is met in his advance by a fourth figure whom we only see in part, his right side having been almost completely cut away. He is fronting us, however—his feet planted firmly on the ground, his right hand folded on his breast, while with his left he grasps the forelock of the impetuous figure of the winged wheels and balances. Thanks to the happy discovery by Professor Cattaneo of part of the fragment missing to the design, we know that a woman's figure stood beyond him, holding in her left hand a palm and in her right a crown which she raises to the stalwart conqueror's head. It is a simple but daring and most spirited composition. It seems to belong to a far remoter past than that of the earliest building of Torcello. Professor Cattaneo explains it as an allegory of the passage of Time, who on his winged wheels has already passed one man by, as he stands stroking his beard, while tears and sorrow await him in the form of the woman on his right in mourning guise and posture; the stalwart man on the left is he who faces Time and takes him by the forelock, and for him the crown and palm of victory are in waiting. But Professor Cattaneo seems to give a needlessly limited significance to the idea of Time. It is to him the Time which God offers to man that he may do what is just and combat his own evil passions; this seems to him to be expressed by the scales and the stick he grasps in his hand. Perhaps it is enough to think merely of the club as that with which a more familiar Time is wont to deal back-handed blows at those who are so idle or so sluggish as to let him pass. At any rate the men of Torcello could comprehend this language of the rough stone. What matter if the oracles were dumb? Which of them had not wept to see the face of Time averted, which of them had not felt the weight of his backward blow? And yet this symbol of old Time must have been mute to them before the great solemn Madonna in the dusky, golden circle of the apse; she looks beyond all fortunes and vicissitudes of man. How should they dare to pray to her? Worship they may, and rise with strength to contend with Time and conquer him, with a weapon to face the mystery of life; but they meet here no smile of comfort, no companionable grace. To those men who dreamed this figure, to us who look upon her and worship, the dominion of Time is a forgotten thing; we ask no pity for our human woes; they have passed, they have crumbled: she gives us a better gift than pity, insight into the hidden things of life and of art; she wings with hope, if with stern hope, our dream of beauty. The mosaics on the west wall of the cathedral have the same stern character, with less of beauty than the Madonna of the apse: the great angels on either side the weird central Christ in the upper division have a strangely oriental effect. They might be Indian gods. They hold the Christian symbols, but with how abstracted, how remote a gaze they look out from their aureoles! They are at one with the noble simplicity and strength and greatness of the spirit of the building they adorn. Somehow they seem to us the oldest thing within it; we begin to be drawn by them into mysteries older than the caves of Greece whence the pillars of this duomo came; we begin to share their watch over a vast desert where all the faiths and imaginings of men may move and mingle, and find a common altar under the dome of the evening sky.

Greater than Torcello, and still maintaining, as near neighbour to Venice, something of its old activities, Murano lives, none the less, a phantom life. We would choose, as a fitting atmosphere for Murano, a day of delicate lights and pale, lucent water, with faint fine tints within the water and the sky: a day of the falling year, not expectant, only acceptant, pausing in the dim quiet of its decay. Even the hot sunshine, though it irradiates the features of Murano, cannot penetrate to that spent heart. The marvellous fascination of its Grand Canal, with its swift and unaccustomed current of blue waters, cannot draw us from the sadness, or disperse the spectral melancholy which invades the spirit and surrounds it as an atmosphere. The sun infects the dirty children with a desire to shine, and prompts somersaults for a soldino; but the weary women, the old, crouching men, still creep about the fondamenta impervious to his rays. Murano is not less disinherited, not less phantasmal, because the daylight comes to pierce the semblance of her life. It is strangely invasive and possessing, this sentiment of a life outlived, a body whose soul is fled. The long vine gardens that spread to the lagoon, dispossessed, but still apparently doing service and rich in vegetables and fruit, seem as if they would persuade us of their reality; but their walls are ruined, their ways are low and narrow; it was not thus they looked when Bembo and Navagero paced here in an earthly paradise, a haunt of nymphs and demigods. The living population of Murano seems to have fallen under the same spell. If we bestow on them more than a cursory glance as we pass along the fondamenta, we seem to detect in their faces an indescribable sense of weariness and sorrow and decay. There seem many old among them, and on the young toil and privation have already laid their hand. The strange habitual chant of priest and women and young girls, going up from tired nerveless throats in the twilight of San Pietro Martire, seemed a symbol of the voice of Murano, melancholy, mechanical, the phantom of a voice—an echo struck with the hand or by a breath of wind from a fallen instrument, an instrument that has lost its virtue and its ring, an instrument unstrung. We have seen Murano in festa. She can pay her tribute to free Italy. Ponte Lungo was hung with lamps, and the desolate campi had their share in the illumination. In the very piazza of San Donato a hawker was winding elastic strings of golden treacle, while women and children in gay dresses hurried to and fro. In another square, under the clock tower, a demagogue addressed the crowd excitedly: there was plentiful noise, plentiful determination to enjoy. The campanile looked down and wondered. *O Roma o morte*. Had it been Rome then and not death? Rome and freedom, freedom to destroy the historic and the old? It was a grand triumph, a triumph justly commemorated, and yet the conquerors themselves might grieve over the Italy of to-day. Mazzini, we know, struck a note of melancholy out of that proud exultation. Italy, if she lives, lives among ruins, and for the most part she is careless of her decay.

THE CLOCK TOWER.

Murano, like Torcello, is bound by one glorious link with her Byzantine past, and this one of the noblest monuments, not of the lagoons only, but of all Italy; simple, stern, august. San Donato has not, indeed, gone unscathed by time, nor by modernity. The wonders of its pavement are becoming blackened and obscured; holes are being worn in it, missing cubes leave gaps in the design. In winter it is constantly flooded by high tide, and even in other seasons the damp is ruining a pavement which rivals, if it does not surpass, that of San Marco. It is impossible to describe the beauty of the designs, the exquisite harmonics of its precious marbles, porphyry and verd-antique, Verona, serpentine and marmo greco, with noble masses of colour among the smaller fragments, and a most precious gem of chalcedony, which, if we may believe the poor old sacristan, whose complaints concerning his precious floor wake no response, an English visitor would have wished to steal. The sacristan can show to all who will lament with him the ruin wrought by sacrilegious man. But no profane hand has dared to raise itself against the Madonna of the apse. This Madonna of San Donato is even grander, more august, than that other who in Torcello conquers Time, and surely it is not without reason that we have called her the goddess of the lagoons. In perfect aloofness and secrecy she stands, but with luminous revelation in her strangely significant eyes; her white hands uplifted, her white face shining out of the darkness, the long, straight folds of her dark robe worked with gold, her feet resting, it seems, upon a golden fire. The gaze of this marvellous Madonna seems to comprehend the world. She is a sphinx who holds the key of every mystery. In her presence we are overcome by the impulse to kneel and worship. She is not, like many Byzantine Madonnas, grotesque, forbidding in her immensity, in her aloofness; for even while she rebukes and subdues our littleness of soul, she draws all our senses as a being of absolute, inexplicable beauty. She holds us rapt and will not let us go. The memory of the Duomo of San Donato is concentrated in the single magical figure of her Madonna, leaning in benediction from the golden apse.

Murano is full of corners where Gothic and Byzantine have combined to beautify portico, pillar and arch. In the Asilo dei Vecchii are two of the most ancient fireplaces known in Venice, and at Venice fireplaces were very early in use. One is a deep square hollowed in the wall, and furnished with doors that shut upon it like a panelling, while two little windows, as usual, open out behind. The other projects into the room, with sloping roof and little seats within on either side. Murano, it is well known, was the pleasure-ground of the Venetians in happier days; it was here that the men of the Great Republic had their gardens elect for solace and for beauty. But with the Republic Murano fell; the patrimonies of the patricians were scattered—gradually their palaces were snatched away, piece by piece, and fell into irrecoverable ruin. One only now retains some image of its former splendour, the famous Cà da Mula, upon the fine sweep of the Grand Canal. The Madonna of San

Donato has looked down on the spoliation of her temple; she still looks on its slow decay. She has shared the proud sorrows of the campanile; in colloquy through the night what may he not have told of the passing of Murano? They have little, these solemn guardians of the past, in common with the exuberant Renaissance, but perhaps a common fate, the unifying hand of Time, may have bound their spirits in a confraternity of grief. The heart of the old campanile would be stirred with pity for the fate of those deserted palaces, the sublime Madonna would turn an eye not of scorn but of sorrow on the fading forms of those radiant women, so splendid on the frescoed palace fronts, so alluring in the smooth mirror of the canal. The work of the spoiler, so far as it was a work of violence, of a human spoiler, is done; but the slower work of nature still proceeds.

Long before Murano became a Venetian pleasure-ground, she had been famous for her painters, for her ships, for her furnaces. Like Torcello, she sent vessels to the triumph of the Doge Lorenzo Tiepolo, and she was conspicuous among the others, as da Canale says: "For you must know that those of Murano had on their vessels living cocks, so that they might be known and whence they came." Molmenti thinks that Carpaccio himself belonged to a shipbuilding family of Murano, and this is the more interesting in view of the frequency and detail of shipping operations in his pictures. Murano was indeed the birthplace of Venetian art, and the riches of its furnaces glow in the garments of those early painters, Vivarini, Andrea and Quirico. From the end of the eleventh century the glass works had begun to flourish; by the thirteenth the industry was transferred wholly to Murano. The legend runs that a certain Cristoforo Briani, hearing from Marco Polo of the monopoly of agates, chalcedony and other precious stones on the coast of Guiana, set about imitating them. With Domenico Miotto to help him he succeeded, and the latter carried the art to still greater perfection, which resulted at last in the imitation of the pearl. In 1528 Andrea Vidoare received a special mariegola or charter for the fame of his wonderful pearls, polished and variegated by him to a degree unknown before. In the middle of the fifteenth century the first crystals came from the furnaces, and the following century was the golden period of the art—a period coinciding with the greatest patrician glory of the island. Murano still burns with its secular fire, winning from the old world its secrets, the old, wise world that worshipped fire, to fuse them once more in its crucible for the wonder of the new; secrets of crystal, pearl and ruby, and of the blue of the deepest ocean depths or the impenetrable night sky, imprisoning them in those transparent cenotaphs in forms of infinite harmony and grace. And it is not only in the revival of ancient memories and forgotten mysteries that the furnaces of Murano play their part; they contribute also to the present renewal of Venice: for it is here that the units of the mosaicist's art are made. In Murano is laid the foundation-stone of its success—the quality of the colour, the depth and richness of the gold. The period of decadence in the Venetian arts is accurately reflected in its mosaics; with the decadence of conception we note also the decadence of colour. Those hard blatant tones that characterise the late mosaics of San Marco are records, too permanent, alas! of a time when the furnaces had lost their cunning, or rather when the master minds were blunted and the secret of the ancient colourists allowed to lie unquestioned under the dust of time.

There is a humbler department of the glass works which we must not pass by. It lies away from the furnaces devoted to rare and subtle texture and design, behind San Pietro Martire, among the gardens: a manufactory of common glass for daily use, tumblers and water-bottles and other humble ware. Here there is the swift operation of machinery, at least among the coarser glasses, and a noise of the very inferno with countless sweating fiends—little black-faced grinning boys, grateful for a package full of grapes or juicy figs; there is little mystery in the production of this coarser glass, or rather few of the obvious accessories of mystery, the delicate slow fashioning, the infusion of colours. Instead, the constant noise of machinery, deafening and exhausting in its incessant motion, though even here the reign of machinery is limited: the finer tumblers must go a longer journey to be filed by a slower, more gradual process, the direct handiwork of man. There is an upper circle to which we gladly pass from this inferno, almost a paradise if we contrast it with the turmoil and heat below; to reach it we pass by the troughs of grey sand which all day men are trampling with the soles of their bare feet, to mould into fit temper for the furnace. The floor of the room above is covered and the walls lined with strange creations of cold, grey earth, fashioned by hand, roll after roll of clay, ungainly forms to be inhabited by fire. This upper attic, with its company of mute grey moulds, opens out upon the vineyards of Murano, with water shimmering through the long golden alleys, and the city visible beyond. The gardens of the Palazzo da Mula and of San Cipriano are beside us. The bustle of the new world has invaded the peaceful seclusion of a spot once sacred to the student aristocracy of Venice.

For this island, famed for so glorious an industry, was beloved and honoured by the noblest of Venetian names, Trifone Gabriele and Pietro Bembo and Andrea Navagero. Here Navagero founded one of the first botanic gardens of Europe—"a terrestrial paradise, a place of nymphs and demigods"; here Gabriele wandered for hours under the thick vine pergola walled with jessamine against the sun. And it was not only as a temporary pleasure-ground that they loved Murano: they clung to it as their resting-place in death. Bernardo Giustiniani desired to be buried by his palace, at the foot of Ponte Lungo, and Andrea Navagero in the church of San Martino in the same quarter where his house was built. Murano was honoured by at least one royal guest. It was here that Henry III of France, on his passage through Venice from Polonia, was given his first lodging, and the palace which witnessed the first transports of this rapturous monarch, the palace of Bartolomeo Capello, still exists, close beside the church of Santa Maria degli Angeli, at the extreme western point of the city. It would thus form the most convenient landing-place, besides commanding a view of extreme beauty; to the left, the fine torrent-like sweep of the chief canal, with the noble Cà da Mula a little lower on the opposite bank and its gardens immediately over the water; Venice filling the horizon clear across the lagoon, where the south curve of Murano ends to-day in a meadow of rough grass and fragrant herbs; to the right the Convent of the Angeli, leading on the eye across the lagoon to the mainland and the distant mountains beyond. Traces of fresco remain on the outer walls of the palazzo, and the upper hall still stretches through the whole breadth of the house. It is on the balcony of this central hall that Henry must have stood when he appeared before dinner to gratify the crowds on the fondamenta and in the boats below. The view of Venice in the evening light is exquisitely lovely, with the lagoon spread like a mirror to reflect the delicate opaline of the sunset sky. In this hall hung with cloth of gold and cremosine, and perhaps with the colours of Veronese, looking over a paradise of gardens and water to the immortal city, Henry kept his court, received the legates from the Pope and said a thousand graceful things about His Holiness, rejoiced the natives by his noble bearing, his perfumed gloves, his frank pleasure in their tribute, his decision to go on foot to the Angeli to morning Mass. Thus was he initiated to the magical city and its enchantments by that wise providence of the Venetians, who made their islands always stepping-stones, outer courts of the central shrine, where their pilgrim must pause awhile to shake the dust of the mainland off his feet, that the spell might permeate his being and fill his senses with desire.

The fondamenta below Henry's palace, leading to the church of the Angeli, is one of the most desolate in Murano; the wide green campo of the cemetery which opens from it is deserted and bare, save for a few fowls that humbly commemorate the proud old shield. The dirt of the children is indescribable, as they press close begging a soldino. But their dirt is dearer to them. A bargain for a washed face, even when the reward rings cheerily on the pavement, brings no response but laughter and surprise. We are reminded by contrast of the tribute of Andrea Calmo, a popular poet of the sixteenth century:

E voio tanto bene a quel Muran,

Che, per diroelo certo in veritæ,

Son in pensier de vender le mie intræ.

E venir la per starmene pì san.

Quei horti a pieni de herbe uliose

E quel canal cusi chiaro e pulio

Con quelle belle casi si aierose,

Con tante creature che par riose

Liogo che l'ha stampao Domenedio.

(And I wish so well to that Murano, that to tell you the sober truth I am thinking of selling my takings and coming there to live more healthily. The gardens there are so full of olive trees, and the canal so clear and clean, the houses so beautiful and so airy, with so many fair creatures that it seems a place of joy stamped by the Lord God.) Beside the Cà da Mula, hidden among some outbuildings, from which it has in the last years been partially released, is one of Murano's finest treasures, the convent front of San Cipriano, which in the ninth century, when Malamocco was on the point of submersion, was brought here by order of Ordelafo Faliero. Andrea Dandolo dates the building from 881; it was rebuilt in 1109 and restored in 1605, and its exquisite façade, still bearing the stamp of several ages, freed somewhat from the earth about its base, stands up nobly from the tangled garden around it. The central arch is outlined with the finest Byzantine tracery lined with Gothic, surrounded once with coloured marbles of which only fragments now remain, and above this is a frieze of the best Roman of the Renaissance: slender columns, some Byzantine, some Gothic, adorn it on either side, and fantastic Byzantine symbols are sculptured in the stone discs that are embedded in the walls between the arches of the cloister. A campanula on the ruined wall to the left of the arch stands out clear and pale against the brick building behind, where once the cloister opened out, an exquisite harmony of lavender and rose. Fragmentary though it is, this façade of the famous monastery is one of the most precious relics of the islands of the lagoons.

There is an island where we cannot think of death, where decay dare not come; though the water plants smell faint upon its shores, and the cypresses that clothe it rise black against the sky. It is the island that sheltered one of the most joyful spirits that has ever walked the world, the island where the larks once sang in such prolonged impulsive harmony of joy that the sound of their singing has never passed away; it may seem to lie silent as a veil upon the water, but the tremor of the sunshine will waken it to renewed harmonics of delight—San Francesco del Deserto. We rejoice to think that the Poverello set foot in the lagoons, that he left here in the lonely waters the blossom of his love. St. Francis of the Desert can wake no thoughts of melancholy, and indeed this is no deserted place, nor in the morning of his coming, after the night of storm, can it have seemed a place of desolation; for nothing is more wonderful, more prodigally full of the mysterious rapture of life, than the flowing in of day upon the lagoons after the tumult of rain and hurricane. They say that St. Francis, coming from the Holy Land on a Venetian ship, was driven by the storm to cast anchor near Torcello; that as he prayed, the storm subsided, and a great calm fell on the lagoon. Then as the

Poverello set foot upon this cypress-covered shore, the sun came out—the sun of the early summer dawn—and shone through the dripping branches of the cypresses, covering them with glistening crystals, and shone on the damp feathered creatures among the branches and on the larks among the reedy grass, and as he shone a choir of voices woke in the lonely island and a chorus of welcome burst from ten thousand throats. And the sun shone in the heart of St. Francis also, and it overflowed with joy; and St. Francis said to his companion, "The little birds, our brothers, praise their Creator with joy; and we also as we walk in the midst of them—let us sing the praises of God." And then as St. Bonaventura relates the legend, the birds sang so clamorously on the branches that St. Francis had to entreat their silence till he had sung the Lauds; but we may read another story if we will, and say that the dewy matin song of the birds was not so clamorous as to disturb the quiet morning gladness of the Poverello, that they sang together in the dawn. San Francesco del Deserto is not an island of sorrow. In the little convent inhabited still by a few quiet Franciscans, the narrow gloomy corner is to be seen which they name St. Francis's bed: in the convent garden there rises a stone memorial round the tree that flowered from the Saint's planted staff. We know these familiar symbols of the Franciscan convents: the brothers cling to them as to some fragmentary testament that their eyes can read and their hand grasp when the living spirit has fled away; everywhere among the mountain or the valley solitudes where St. Francis dwelt, the same dark relics of that luminous spirit are to be found, the story even of birds banished for ever by the command of that prince of singers, as if his own voice chanting eternal litanies could be his sole delight. They are strange stories; we pass them by, and go out to find the Poverello where the cones of the cypresses gleam silver-grey against the blue. His spirit has taken happy root among the waters of the lagoons; a new joy and glory is added to the mountains as they rise in the calm dawn, clear and luminous from the departing rain cloud; there is joy and peace in the raised grass walk between the cypress trees; the island is indeed a place of life and not of death for those who have felt the suffering and the joy of love, and who worship beauty in their hearts.

O Beata Solitudo,

O Sola Beatitudo.

There are still solitudes in the desert of the lagoon where some of us have dreamed of beginning a new day. In the hour when the last gold has faded from the sun-path—when those dancing gems he flings to leap and sport upon the water have been slowly gathered in, when the churches and palaces of the city are folded under one soft clinging veil, which softens the outline that it does not obscure, when Torcello and Burano lean in pallid solitude above the level disc of the marsh, and the Lido lies like a sea-serpent coiled on itself, its spires reflected in the motionless mirror far south to Chioggia—they steal out, these island phantoms, faint, alluring, upon the still mosaic of the lagoon, like black pearls in that shell-like surface of tenderest azure and rose. Shall we not dare to wander among those lovely paths, those dimly burning gems? None visits them, unless it be the golden stars and the dreaming lover of Endymion: their roof is the broad rainbow spread above them by the setting sun. They seem sometimes to welcome a spirit that should come and dwell among them silently; one that should tread them with loving reverence and quiet hope, seeking to set free the fantasies with which earth has stored it, but which no power of earth may help it to disburden.

Chapter Three
THE NUPTIALS OF VENICE

UNTIL the fall of the Venetian Republic the rite of the *Sporalizio del Mare*, the wedding of Venice with the sea, continued to be celebrated annually at the feast of the Ascension. Long after the fruits of the espousal had been gathered, when its renewal had become no more than a ceremonious display, there stirred a pulse of present life in the embrace; and in a sense, the significance of the ceremony never can be lost while one stone remains upon another in the city of the sea.

For the earliest celebration of the nuptials there was need of no golden Bucintoro, no feast of red wine and chestnuts, no damask roses in a silver cup, not so much as a ring to seal the bond. For it was no vaunt of sovereignty; it was a humble oblation, a prayer to the Creator that His creature might be calm and tranquil to all who travelled over it, an oblation to the creature that it might be pleased to assist the gracious and pacific work of its Creator. The regal ceremony of later times was inaugurated by the Doge Pietro Orseolo II who, having largely increased the sea dominion of Venice and made himself lord of the Adriatic, welded his achievement into the fabric of the state by the ceremony of the espousal. The ring was not introduced till the year 1177, when Pope Alexander III, being present at the festival, bestowed it on the Doge, as token of the papal sanction of the ceremony, with the words, "Receive it as pledge of the sovereignty that you and your successors shall maintain over the sea." But the true importance of the festival, whether in its primitive form or in its later elaboration, is the development of Venetian policy which it signified—a development which, for the purposes of this chapter, will best be considered in relation to events separated by nearly two centuries, but united in their acknowledgment of the growing importance of Venice on the waters. The first is Pietro Orseolo's Dalmatian campaign, followed in 1001 by the secret visit of the German Emperor Otho III, and the second the famous concordat of Pope Alexander III and the Emperor Frederick Barbarossa, concluded under the auspices of Venetian statecraft in 1177.

Pietro Orseolo II appears as one of the most potent interpreters of the Venetian spirit. He combined qualities which enabled him to gather together the threads which the genius of Venice and the exigencies of her position were weaving, and to fashion from them a substantial web on which her industry might operate. He was a soldier, a great statesman and a patriot. All the subtlety, all the ambition, all the dreams of glory with which his potent and spacious mind was endowed, were at his country's service, and the material in which he had to work was plastic to his touch. Venice lay midway between the kingdoms of the East and West, and from the earliest times this fact had determined her importance: she might rise to greatness or she might be annihilated; she could not be ignored. The Venice of Orseolo was instinct with vitality and teeming with energies, but she was divided against herself. The foundations of her greatness were already laid, but her general aim and tendency were not determined. She was in need of a leader of commanding mind and capacious imagination, who could envisage her future, and who should possess the power of inspiring others with confidence in his dreams. Such a man was Pietro Orseolo II. Venice had been threatened with destruction by the division of the two interests which, interwoven, were the basis of her power. Before the final settlement at Rialto she had been torn hither and thither by the factions of the East and West, the party favouring Constantinople and the party favouring the Frankish King; and at any moment still the Doge's policy might be wrecked by the rivalries of the two parties, if he proved lacking in insight or capacity for uniting in his service the interests of both.

RIVA DEGLI SCHIAVONI.

For some time Dalmatia had been a thorn in the side of Venice, a refuge for the disloyal, and, through the agency of the hordes of pirates infesting the coast, a real menace to her commerce. Venice had attempted to purchase immunity from the pirates by payment of an annual indemnity. Orseolo decided at once to put an end to this payment, but he realised that the price of the decision was a foothold in Dalmatia that would need to be obtained by force of arms. For this end it was necessary to secure harmony within the city itself, and, knowing this, he exercised his powers to obtain approval of his expedition from the authorities of East and of West, from the Emperors of Germany and Byzantium. He was successful in this, and circumstances combined further to aid his designs. The Croatians and Narentines, by wreaking on Northern Dalmatia their anger at the loss of the Venetian indemnity, had prepared the minds of the Dalmatians to look on the prospect of Venetian supremacy as one of release rather than of subjugation. It is said that they even went so far as to send a message to Orseolo encouraging his coming. Their province was nominally under the Emperor of Byzantium, but their overlord had decided to look favourably on a means of securing peace and safe passage to his province at so small an expense to himself. Orseolo set sail on Ascension Day, after a service in the Cathedral of Olivolo (now San Pietro di Castello), fortified by the good will of East and of West, and the united acclamations of all parties in Venice. Pride and vigorous hope must have swelled the hearts of these warriors. It was summer, and their songs must have travelled across the dazzling blue of the great basin of St. Mark, and echoed and re-echoed far out on the crystal waters of the lagoon. Triumph was anticipated, and triumph was their portion. Orseolo's expedition was little less than a triumphal progress; the coast towns of Dalmatia from Zara to Ragusa rendered him their homage. A new and immensely rich province was acquired by Venice, and the title of Duke of Dalmatia accorded to himself.

Soon after Orseolo's return from this campaign, Venice, unknown to herself, was to receive the homage of one of the emperors she had made it her business to propitiate. There is something that stirs the imagination in this secret visit of Otho III to the Doge. According to the ingenuous account of John the Deacon, Venetian ambassador at the Emperor's court, it was merely one of those visits of princely compliment which the age knew so well how to contrive, and loved so well to recount—a visit in disguise for humility or greater freedom, like that of St. Louis to Brother Giles at Perugia, where host and guest embrace in fellowship too deep for words. The Emperor, John the Deacon tells us, was overcome with admiration of Orseolo's achievements in Dalmatia, and filled with longing to see so great a man, and the chronicler was despatched to Venice to arrange a meeting. The Doge, while acknowledging the compliment of Otho's message, could not believe in its reality, and consequently kept his own counsel about it—"tacitus sibi in corde servabat." However, when Otho on his travels had come down to Ravenna for Lent, John the Deacon was again despatched, and this time from Doge to Emperor.

It was ultimately arranged that after the Easter celebration Otho with a handful of followers should repair, under pretext of a "spring-cure," to the abbey of Santa Maria in the isle of Pomposa at the mouth of the Po. He pretended to be taking up his quarters here for several days, but at nightfall he secretly embarked in a small boat prepared by John the Deacon, and set sail with him and six followers for Venice. All that night and all the following day the little boat battled with the tempest, and the storm was still unabated the next evening, when it put in at the island of San Servolo and found itself harboured at last in the waters of St. Mark. Venice knew nothing of this arrival; her royal guest had taken her unawares, and her waterways had prepared him no welcome. We may picture the anxiety of Orseolo, alone with the secret of his expected guest, on the island of San Servolo. The journey may well have been perilous for so small a boat even within the sheltering wall of the Lido, and we may imagine his relief when it could at last be descried beating towards the island through the tempestuous waters of the lagoon. In impenetrable night, concealed from one another's eyes by the thick darkness, Emperor and Doge embraced. Otho was invited to rest for an hour or two at the convent of San Zaccaria, but he repaired before dawn to the Ducal Palace and the lodging made ready for him in the eastern tower. There is a fascination in attempting to imagine the two sovereigns moving amid the shadows of Venetian night, in thinking of the Emperor watching from the vantage of his tower for daybreak over the city. There are wonders to be seen from this eastern aspect, but after the discomfort of his voyage to Venice the royal captive may well have felt a longing for a sight of the city from within. It is all rather like a children's game—Orseolo's feigned first meeting with an embassy from Otho, his inquiry as to the Emperor's health and whereabouts, and the public dinner with the ambassadors. Venice is robbed of a pageant, and one most dear to her, the fêting of a royal guest; the guest is deprived of all festivities beyond a christening of the Doge's daughter; yet the pleasurable excitement of John the chronicler communicates itself and disarms our criticism; and it is not till gifts have been offered and refused—"ne quis cupiditatis et non Sancti Marci tuæque dilectionis causa me hac venisse asserat"—till tears and kisses have been exchanged, and the Emperor, this time preceding his companions by a day, has set sail once more for the island of Pomposa, that we break from the spell of the chronicler and begin to cavil at the strange conditions of the visit.

Modern historians have laid a probing hand on the sentimentality of John the Deacon's tale; they do not doubt the kisses or the tears, but the unparalleled eccentricity of secrecy seems to demand an urgent motive. Why this strange coyness of the Emperor? Might he not have thought more to honour Venice and her Doge by coming with imperial pomp than by stealing in and out of the triumphant city like a thief in the night? And why did the persons concerned make public boast of the success of their freak immediately after its occurrence? For John tells us that when three days had passed, the people were assembled by the Doge at his palace to hear of his achievement, "and praised no less the faith of the Emperor than the skill of their leader." The probable solution of the various enigmas rather rudely shatters the romance. Gfrörer lays on Orseolo the responsibility of the *incognito*, attributing it partly to a memory of the fate that overtook the Candiani's personal relations with an imperial house, partly to his desire to treat with the Emperor unobserved. He recalls point by point the precautions taken by Orseolo to preclude Otho from contact with other Venetians, and comes to the conclusion that in those private interviews in the tower the "eternal dreamer" was feasted on the milk and honey of promises, food of which no third person could have been allowed to partake. "What lies," he exclaims, "were invented, what assurances vouchsafed of the most unbounded devotion to imperial projects in general and the longed-for reconstitution of the Roman Empire in particular! Never was prince so shamefully abused as Otho III at Venice." It is not necessary to abandon our belief in Otho's personal feelings for the Doge, augmented by Orseolo's recent campaign, to realise that there must have been another side to the picture. Gulled the royal guest in all probability was, but there is little doubt that he had an axe of his own to be ground on this visit to Venice—that the journey had for its aim something beyond his delectation in a sight of the Doge and his obeisance to the Lion. For the furtherance of his schemes of empire Otho needed a fleet. He had, Gfrörer tells us, "an admiral already in view for it. Nothing was wanted but cables, anchors, equipments; in short there were not even ships, nor the necessary money, and above all, there were no sailors. I believe that Otho III undertook the journey to Venice precisely to procure for himself these necessary trifles. Who knows how many times already he had urged the Doge to hasten his sending of the long-promised fleet; but in place of ships nothing had yet come but letters or embassies carrying specious excuses." If the historian's motivisation is accurate, Otho must have found, like so many after him, Venice more capable of exercising persuasion than of submitting to it. For our uses, however, the original or the revised versions of the tale serve the same purpose. As an act of spontaneous homage or an act of practical policy, the visit of Otho, full as it is of speculative possibilities, was an imperial tribute to the position Orseolo had given to Venice, an imperial recognition of her progress towards supremacy in the Adriatic.

Orseolo's achievement and the rite which symbolised it were confirmed two centuries later when, in the spring and summer of 1177, Venice was the meeting place of Pope Alexander III and the Emperor Frederick Barbarossa. Tradition has woven a curious romance round the fact of the Pope's sojourn in Venice before the coming of the Emperor. By a manipulation of various episodes, he is brought as a fugitive to creep among the tortuous by-ways of the city, sleeping on the bare ground, and going forward as chance might direct till he is received as a chaplain—or, to enhance the thrill of agony, as a scullion—in the convent of Santa Maria della Carità, and after some months have elapsed is brought to the notice of the Doge, when a transformation scene of the Cinderella type is effected. It is inevitable that melodramatic touches should have been added to so important an episode, and the accounts of the manner of Alexander's arrival and his bearing in Venice are many and varied. None the less, it is clear that splendour and not secrecy, ceremony not intimacy, are the general colouring of the event. Frederick had shown himself disposed to make peace and to accept the mediation of Venice, and in the early days of the Pope's visit the Venetians had acted as counsellors, pending the agreement as to a meeting place. Significant terms are used by the chroniclers to account for the ultimate choice, and the note which they strike is repeated again and again in the chorus of praise that throughout the centuries was to wait upon Venice. "Pope and Emperor sent forth their mandates to divers parts of the world, that Archbishops, Bishops, Abbots, Ecclesiastics and secular Princes should repair to Venice; for Venice is safe for all, fertile and abounding in supplies, and the people quiet and peace-loving." Secure among the lagoons, Venice is aloof from the disturbances of the mainland cities, and though her inhabitants are proved warriors they are peaceable citizens. Many of the glories of Gentile Bellini's *Procession of the Cross* would be present in the procession in which the Doge and the magnates of Venice formally conducted Alexander III to the city—patriarch, bishops, clergy, and finally the Pope himself, all in their festival robes. Ecclesiastical and secular princes of Germany, France, England, Spain, Hungary and the whole of Italy were crowding to Venice. The occasion gave scope for her fascinations, and they were exerted. No opportunity for display was neglected; ceremony was heaped upon ceremony.

For over a fortnight Venice was the centre of correspondence daily renewed between Emperor and Pope, of embassies hastening to and fro, of endless postponements and uncertainties. The Pope retires for a few days to Ferrara; then he is back again to be received as before. But Venice, the indomitable, is secure of her will, and preparations for the coming of the Emperor are growing apace. In July the Doge's son is despatched to meet the royal guest at Ravenna and conduct him to Venice by way of Chioggia. No tempests disturbed his arrival. He was conducted in triumph up the lagoon by the galleys of "honest men" and Cardinals who had gone forth to Chioggia to meet him. Slowly the islands of the Lido would unfold themselves to his eyes, Pellestrina in shining curves, Malamocco with its long reaches of bare shore and reeds. The group clustered round Venice itself—San Servolo, La Grazia, San Lazzaro, Poveglia—would be green and smiling then, living islands, not desolated as now for the most part by magazine or asylum. San Nicolo del Lido welcomed the guest, and he was borne thence on the ducal boat to the city and landed at the Riva. Through the acclamations of an "unheard-of multitude" his way was made to San Marco, where the Pope in all his robes, amid a throng of gorgeous ecclesiastics and laymen, was waiting on the threshold. As he passed out of the brilliant and garish day into the solemn mosaiced glory of San Marco and moved to the high altar between Pope and Doge singing a Te Deum, "while all gave thanks to God, rejoicing and exulting and weeping," even an emperor and a Barbarossa may well have surrendered his pride. Even we, spectators removed by time, find ourselves exalted on the tide of colour and of sound, and crying to the Venetians, with the strangers who thronged in their streets, "Blessed are ye, that so great a peace has been able to be established in the midst of you! This shall be a memorial to your name for ever." Peace was secured and Venice had accomplished her task. She had devoted the subtleties of her statecraft to its performance, but perhaps the splendour of this hour in San Marco was her crowning achievement. She asked the recognition of a Pope, and she brought the temporal sovereign to his side in a church which is one of the wonders of Christendom. She polished and gilded every detail of her worldly magnificence, and poured it as an oblation at the altar. Her reinforcements to the cause of Alexander III were drawn from far back in the ages, from the inspiration of the men who had fashioned her temple; and may there not be some deeper signification than merely that of Frederick's stubbornness in the "Not to thee, but to St. Peter," traditionally attributed to him as he prostrated himself at his enemy's feet?

THE DOORWAY OF SAN MARCO.

To Venice there remained, beside the praise of all Christendom, many tangible tokens of the events of the summer. Emperor and Pope vied with each other in evincing their gratitude. Alexander formally sanctioned and confirmed the title of Venice as sovereign and queen of the Adriatic, and bestowed on the Doge a consecrated ring for use at the Nuptials. And henceforth the ceremony at San Nicolo del Lido, the place of arrival and departure for the high seas and for Dalmatia and the East, was increased in magnificence. No trace now remains of the church where the rites were performed; but the grassy squares of San Nicolo and the wooded slopes of its canal, looking on one side to the city, on the other to the sea, are beautiful still. The ocean calls to the lagoon, and the calm waters of the lagoon sway themselves in answer; while, outside the Lido, line beyond line of snowy-crested waves, ever advancing, bear in to Venice, Bride of the Adriatic, the will of the high sea.

Chapter Four
VENICE IN FESTIVAL

THE treaty signed in 1573 between Venice and Constantinople, though it marked no real rise in her fortunes, gave her a respite from the petty and fruitless warfare with the Turk, in which she had so long been engaged. That conflict had drained the resources of the Republic without affording compensating gains. The loss and horrors of Famagosta might seem to have been revenged by the battle of Lepanto, where the triumph of Venice and her allies was complete; but owing to the dilatoriness and inaction of Don John of Austria, brother of Philip of Spain, the opportunity of annihilating the Turkish forces was allowed to escape, and victory was reduced to little more than the name. So flagrant had been the character of Don John's disloyalty that the Venetians no longer could mistake his intentions. Spain was an ally of Venice; but Tommaso Morosini was but voicing the general conviction when he exclaimed, "We must face the fact that there will be no profitable progress, seeing that the victory already gained by the forces of the League against the Turk was great in the number of ships captured, rare in the number of slaves set free, famous by reason of the power it broke, formidable for the numbers killed by the sword, glorious for the pride it laid low, terrible in the fame acquired by it. And, none the less, no single foot of ground was gained. Oh, incomparable ignominy and shame of the allies, that whatever honour they obtained in consequence of the victory, they lost by not following it up!" Though nominally in league with her against the Turk, Spain, owing to her jealousy of Venice, was unwilling that the war should be ended. The League of Cambray, formed in 1508 by the European powers unfriendly to Venice, should have made it clear to the Republic that she had over-reached her own interests by interference in the politics of Europe. Moreover, a severe blow had been dealt to the commerce of Venice by the discovery of the Cape route to the East. Yet, though her decline had begun, she still formed a subject for envy, and there is justice in Morosini's conclusion as to the causes of the growing enmity of Spain. "Ruling," he says of the Spaniards, "a good part of Europe, having passed into Africa, having discovered new territory, dominating most of Italy, and seeing the Republic, the single part, the only corner of Italy, to be free and without the least burden of slavery, they envy it, envying it they hate it, and hating it they lay snares for it."

Though the terms of the peace with Constantinople were humiliating in the extreme (Venice relinquished the whole of Cyprus, a fortress in Albania, and agreed within three years to pay an indemnity of one hundred thousand ducats) it set her hands free for awhile and gave her a breathing space in which to return to her pageants. And for the next few years she laid herself out more completely than ever before to impress the world by her splendour. It is not easy to determine the beginnings of decadent luxury in Venetian history. Venice had always been a pleasure-house, a place of entertainment for kings and emperors, a temple of solemn festival. Perhaps the broad difference between the splendours of the early and late Renaissance is that one achieved that perfection of taste which robes luxury in apparent simplicity, while the other was more obvious and expansive—the difference between the Madonnas of Bellini and of Titian, between the interiors of Carpaccio and Paul Veronese. There is a real and discernible difference in aspect between Venice of the fifteenth and Venice of the sixteenth century, but it is not the difference between asceticism and luxury. Venice was never ascetic, no prophet ever drew her citizens round a sacrificial bonfire on the Piazza. On the other hand it is said that a Venetian merchant was burnt in effigy on Savonarola's pile because he had attempted to purchase some of the doomed Florentine treasures. In the course of the fifteenth century isolated voices were indeed raised in protest against the luxury of Venice, and the authorities themselves, as the State coffers grew empty, tried by oratorical appeal and detailed legislation to curb the extravagance of private citizens. But their protests were, in the main, quite ineffectual. Venice could not resist the influences that wove for her each day a magical dress; she could not refuse the treasures of the East: it was her function to be beautiful, to accept and love every wonder, to turn her face against nothing that could glorify. She had always appeared as a miracle to men, she had always lavished her treasures on her guests; the vital difference between the period of her decline and that of her greatness lies in the gradual relaxation of the ties binding her to the sources of her wealth. With the ebbing of her trade her citizens begin to barter their landed estates and their treasures. Morosini's acute and interesting prophecy as to the private banks into which Venetian money began to be diverted provides us with a background to some of the almost fabulous expenditure of the Cinquecento—"The banker," he says, "with a chance of obliging many friends in their need, and acquiring others by such a service, and with power to do so without spending money, simply by making a brief entry, is easily persuaded to satisfy many. When the opportunity arises of buying some valuable piece of furniture or decoration, clothes, jewels and similar things of great price, he is easily persuaded to please himself, simply ordering a line or two to be written in his books—reassuring, or rather, deceiving himself with the thought that one year being passed in this way, he can carry time forward, and pass many years in the same manner, scheming that such an affair or such an investment as he has in hand, when it has come to perfection, ought to prove most useful, and that through its means he may be able to remedy other disorders; which hope proving fallacious shows with how little security walks one who places his thoughts and hopes in the uncertain and inconstant issues of events."

The fabric of sixteenth-century Venice was too largely founded on the "uncertain and inconstant issues of events," but none the less it was as radiant a fabric as any that man has yet fashioned. Something at least of its nature may be learned from the details of the entertainment of Henry III in Venice, and his lodging and reception in the then fashionable suburb of Murano. Henry came to Venice in the early summer of 1574, on his way from Poland to take possession of the throne of France vacated by the death of his brother Charles IX. He came at a moment when Venice was rich in artists to do him honour—Tintoretto, Paolo Veronese, Palladio and Claudio Merulo: he was crowned with the laurels of war; while the Republic was able to clothe herself in the glory of Lepanto and the respite of her newly concluded peace with the Turk and, superficially at least, appeared peculiarly fitted to welcome him. The young King was gracious, and greedy to drink his fill of life, and Venice was unique in her celebration. The visit was one of the most spontaneous, the most joyful to host and guest, of any that are recorded in her annals. All the territory of Venice was prepared to honour him, and his journey was a triumphal progress. There is something joyous still about the little inland cities of his route, echoes of festival still linger in their streets, romance still dwells in their hearts. At Treviso, where the young King was welcomed with peculiar pomp, the Lion of St. Mark, portrayed by three successive ages, rules still, his majesty sustained by the sturdiness of life that moves in the city. The winding cobbled streets are full of bustle and interchange, the arcades are full of people, vital and busily employed. Treviso is not a museum. Its ancient palace of the Cavallieri is still in use, though its loggia with traces of rich fresco is filled with lumber. But we are not critical of small details at Treviso; we thank it for its winding streets and for its leaping azure river; we thank it for its countless ancient roofs and painted rafters; for its houses high and low, harmonious though endless in variation, for the remnants of fresco, shadows no doubt of what once they were, but companionable shadows—horses with still distinguishable motions, graceful maidens both of land and sea. These glories are fading but they have substance still, and on a day of mid-autumn we are well able to imagine a kingly procession on the road from Treviso to Mestre. It seems a pageant, a progress of pomp and colour, as we pass between the vineyards and maize fields and the great gardens and pastures of the villas, down the avenue of plane trees set like gold banners on silvery flagstaffs with carpets of fallen leaves at their feet. Behind them are ranked dark cypresses, pale groups of willow, or companies of poplar. And these are often garlanded to their very summits by crimson creepers, and interspersed with statues, not perhaps great in workmanship, but tempered and harmonised into beauty by the seasons. Here and there is a lawn flanked by dark shrubbery, or a terrace ablaze with dahlias and salvia. And, among them, Baron Franchetti of the Cà d'Oro has a home even more worthy of the golden title than is his palace on the shores of the Grand Canal—a place where the sun reveals miraculous hangings in the shrubberies, sumptuously furnished with scarlet and crimson and gold.

VIEW FROM CÀ D'ORO.

Some such festival of colour, in banners and trappings, would
be Henry's preparation for the pageant of the lagoons. For he
was met at Marghera, half way between Mestre and Venice, by
a troop of senators and noblemen and ambassadors, and
escorted to the palace of Bartolomeo Capello at Murano. Of
the young King's lodging at Murano we have spoken
elsewhere—of the hall hung with gold brocade, with golden
baldaquin, green velvet and silk, its entrance guarded by sixty
halberdiers armed for the occasion with gilt spears borrowed
from the chambers of the Council of Ten. Forty noble youths,
in glorious attire, had been told off to wait on the King. But,
"although a most sumptuous supper was prepared, none the
less His Majesty, when the senators were gone, showed himself
a short while at the windows dressed in cloth of gold and silk;
after which he went to supper, and the princes arrived, so that

it was most glorious with abundant supply of exquisite viands and most delicate foods." The hearts of the Venetians were won by the King's beauty and youth, by his delicate person and grave aspect, by his majestic bearing and his eagerness to please and be pleased. He was in mourning for his brother, but his mourning did not shadow Venice by its gloom. "His Majesty appeared in public dressed all in purple (which is his mourning) with a Flemish cloak, a cap on his head in the Italian mode, with long veil and mantle reaching to his feet, slashed jerkin, stockings and leather collar, and a large shirt-frill most becomingly worn, with perfumed gloves in his hand, and wearing on his feet shoes with heels *à la mode française*."

It would be tedious to relate the details of the splendid entertainments that each day were provided for his delectation; of salutes that made the earth and water tremble, of fireworks glowing all night beneath the windows of the Cà Foscari, of the blaze of light from the candles set in every window and cornice and angle of the buildings along the Grand Canal, of the gilded lilies and pyramids and wheels reflected in the water, "so that the canal seemed like another starry sky." It was a veritable gala for Henry; he paid a private visit to the Doge to the great satisfaction of that prince and his senate, he went about *incognito* in a gondola alone with the Duke of Ferrara, "so that when they thought he was in his room, he was in some other part of the city, returning home at an exceedingly late hour accompanied by many torches, and immensely enjoying the liberty of this town; and on account of his charm and courtesy, the whole place gave vent to the lasting joy and satisfaction it felt in continually seeing him." He spent three hours in the Arsenal, engrossed in viewing the vast preparation for war and the spoils won from the Turk "in the sea battle on the day of the great victory"; and then in the chamber of the Council of Ten, within the Arsenal, he was provided with a Sugar Feast, with sugar dishes, knives and forks, so admirably counterfeit that His Majesty only realised their nature when his sugar napkin crumbled and a piece of it fell to the ground. Is there not something contributive to our picture of Venice the entertainer, in this feast of sugar given by the terrible Council of Ten within the walls of the Arsenal itself? There is naturally much vague repetition in the chronicles of the time, but here and there are vital touches which bring the young King to life before our eyes. At the banquet given in his honour in the Sala del Gran Consiglio, having eaten sufficiently himself, he brought the meal to an end before half of the courses had appeared, by adroitly causing the Dukes of Savoy and Ferrara to rise in their places at his side, and calling for water for his hands during the disturbance caused by the lords and ambassadors as they followed the example of the dukes. He told Giovanni Michele that of all the entertainments he had witnessed in Venice none had pleased him more than the "Guerra dei Ponti," and that if he had known of it earlier he would have prayed to have had the spectacle repeated several times, for he "could have asked nothing better than this." The Guerra dei Ponti were wrestling matches that took place on certain bridges over the canals, and pages of description might not have told us as much of the nature of the man who lived behind the scented gloves and purple mantle, as this single expression of preference.

Two episodes in the visit of Henry that seem worthy of fuller record stand out from the rest: his reception at the Lido and the Ball in the Ducal Palace; and they represent the achievements in his honour of two departments of Venetian activity, the City Guilds and the Court. While he was still in his lodging at Murano barges of immense splendour, vying with each other in symbolism and ingenuity of design, and each representing one of the trades of Venice, had arrived to accompany him to the Lido. If we imagine the Lord Mayor's Procession, with splendour a thousandfold enhanced and with drapery and design of artistic excellence, removed from the streets to the glittering surface of the lagoon, we may have some idea of the spectacle. Among the most splendid of the barges was that of the Druggists, with an ensign of the Saviour riding on the world. "The outer coverings themselves were of cloth of gold, and below them and below the oars were painted canvases. The poop was hung within with most beautiful carpets, and on the four sides four pyramids were erected of sky blue with fireworks inside them, at the feet of which were four stucco figures representing four nymphs, and there were set two arquebuses and a musket and two flags white and red and a flag of battle. And on the outside were divers sorts of arms, spears and shields and six arquebuses. On the prow was a pyramid with fireworks, on the top of which was an angel— for this and the Golden Head were the badges of the two honoured druggists who had decked the said vessel—and in the midst of it was a design of a pelican with a motto round it in letters of gold, *Respice Domino*, representing the pelican as wounding its breast to draw blood from it to nourish its offspring, just as they, the druggists, faithful and devoted to their prince and master, gave and offered to him, not only their faculties but their blood itself, which is their own life in his service; and at the foot of the pyramid was a little boy beating a drum." The Looking-Glass Makers also had prepared a magnificent barge glittering with symbols of their profession. But perhaps the device of the Glass-Workers of Murano out-rivalled all others in ingenuity and pomp. "On two great barges, chained together and covered with painted canvases, they had erected a furnace in the form of a sea-monster; and following the train of vessels, flames were seen issuing from its mouths, and, the masters having given their consent, the Glass-Workers made most beautiful vases of crystal, which were cause of great pleasure to the King."

The Convent of Sant' Elena was the vantage point chosen for looking on Venice, and at the moment the army of barges and brigantines reached it, they spread out in front of His Majesty, and a salute broke from them all; "to which the galleys in the train of the King replied in such ordered unity that His Majesty rose to his feet with great curiosity to see them, praising exceedingly so wonderful a sight, admiring to his right the fair and famous city marvellously built upon the salt waters, and on the left a forest of so many ships and vessels with so great noise of artillery and arquebuses, and of trumpets and drums, that he remained astounded; while he openly showed himself not less merry than content, seeing so rare a thing as was never before seen of him." Henry's arrival at the Lido is portrayed in the Sala delle Quattro Porte in the Ducal Palace. He is seen advancing with sprightly step, between two dignitaries of the Church, up a temporary wooden bridge towards the Triumphal Arch and Temple of Palladio. This arch was decorated with paintings by Paolo and Tintoretto, and in connexion with it Ridolfi tells a delightful story of the painting of Henry's portrait. "Tintoretto," says Ridolfi, "was longing to paint the King's portrait, and in consequence begged Paolo to finish the arch by himself; and, taking off his toga, Tintoretto dressed himself as one of the Doge's equerries, and took his place among them in the Bucintoro as it moved to meet the King, thus furtively procuring a chalk sketch of the proposed portrait, which he was afterwards to enlarge to life size; and having made friends with M. Bellagarda, the King's treasurer, he was introduced with much difficulty, owing to the frequent visits of the Doge, into the royal apartments to retouch the portrait from life. Now whilst he stood painting, and the King with great courtesy admiring, there entered presumptuously into the apartments at smith of the Arsenal, presenting an ill-done portrait by himself, and saying that, while His Majesty was dining in the Arsenal, he had done the likeness of him. His presumption was humbled by a courtier who snatched it from his hand, and ripping it up with his dagger threw it into the neighbouring Grand Canal: which incident, on account of the whispering it produced, made it difficult for the painter to carry out his intention. Tintoretto had also observed on that occasion that from time to time certain persons were introduced to the King, whom he touched lightly on the shoulder with his rapier, adding other ceremonies. And pretending not to understand the meaning, he asked it of Bellagarda, who said that they were created knights by His Majesty, and that he, Tintoretto, might prepare himself to receive that degree; for he had discussed the matter with the King, to whom Tintoretto's conditions were known and who had shown himself disposed, in attestation of his powers, to create him also a knight; but our painter, not being willing to subject himself to any title, modestly rejected the offer." When the portrait was finished and presented to the King, it was acclaimed by him as a marvellous likeness, and we may safely conclude from this that it was fair to look on. The King presented it to the Doge. Perhaps the picture from the first had been intended as a present for Mocenigo, and this was the explanation of the secrecy observed in regard to it.

COURTYARD OF PALAZZO DUCALE.

The climax of entertainment was reached in the festa at the Ducal Palace on the second Sunday after Henry's arrival (his visit lasted ten days). The glories of Venice were gathered in that marvellous hall still hung with the paintings of Carpaccio and Gentile Bellini, and the exquisite Paradise of Guariento; for it was yet a year previous to the great fire which was to give scope to the contemporary giants. The later victories of Venice were as yet unchronicled except in the hearts of living men. There was no thought of sumptuary laws on this day at least of the great festival. Ladies were there clothed all in ormesine, adorned with jewels and pearls of great size, not only in strings on their necks, but covering their head-dresses and the cloaks on their shoulders. "And in their whiteness, their beauty and magnificence, they formed a choir not so much of nymphs as of very goddesses. They were set one behind the other in fair order upon carpeted benches stretching round the whole hall, leaving an ample space in the centre, at the head of which was set a royal seat with a covering of gold and entirely covered with a baldaquin from top to bottom, and round it yellow and blue satin." All the splendours of Venetian and Oriental cloths were lavished on the Hall of the Great Council and the Sala del Scrutinio adjoining. The King as usual entered whole-heartedly into the festivity. His seat was raised that he might look over the company, "but he chose nevertheless to go round and salute all the ladies with much grace and courtesy, raising his cap as he went along." After a time musical instruments were heard, the ladies were carried off by the gentlemen, and forming into line they began to dance a slow measure, passing before the King and bowing as they passed. "And he stood the whole while cap in hand." The French courtiers were permitted by their master to lay aside their mourning for the time, and they danced with great merriment, vying with the most famous dancers of Venice. But the great feature of the evening was the tragedy by Cornelio Frangipani—a mythological masque in honour of the most Christian King and of Venice herself—with Proteus, Iris, Mars, Amazons, Pallas and Mercury as protagonists. To the first printed edition of his masque Frangipani prefixed an apology for his title of tragedy, with the usual appeal to classic precedent. "This tragedy of mine," he says, "was recited in such a way as most nearly to approach to the form of the ancients; all the players sang in sweetest harmony, now accompanied, now alone; and finally the chorus of Mercury was composed of players who had so many various instruments as were never heard before. The trumpets introduced the gods on to the appointed scene with the machinery of tragedy, but this could not be used to effect on account of the great concourse of people; and the ancients could not have been initiated into the musical compositions in which Claudio Merulo had reached a height certainly never attained by the ancients." The masque is in reality a mere masque of occasion, comparable to countless English productions in the Elizabethan age, though lacking in the lyrical grace they generally possess. Henry is addressed as the slayer of monsters, the harbinger of peace, the herald of the age of gold—

Pregamo questo domator de' mostri

Ch'eterno al mondo viva,

Perchè in pregiata oliva

Ha da cangiar d' alloro

E apportar l' antica età del' oro.

The masque is without literary merit, but we need not regard it in the cold light of an after day, caged and with clipped wings. To that glorious assembly, illumined by the great deeds fresh in men's minds and the presence of a royal hero, Frangipani's words may well have been kindled into flame. For if time and place were ever in conspiracy to wing pedestrian thoughts and words, it must have been at this fêting of the most Christian King of France in the City of the Sea.

Pens were busy in Venice during the days of Henry's stay. Unsalaried artists, independent of everything except a means of livelihood, exacted toll from the royal guest. From the 16,000 scudi of largess distributed by the King, payments are enumerated "to writers and poets who presented to His Majesty Latin works and poems made in praise of his greatness and splendour." Gifts, as well as compliments were exchanged on all hands. The Duke of Savoy presented the Doge's wife with a girdle studded with thirty gold rosettes each containing four pearls and a precious jewel in the centre, worth 1,800 scudi. And Henry's final token of gratitude to his entertainers was to send after the Doge, who had accompanied him to Fusina, a magnificent diamond ring, begging that Mocenigo should wear it continually in token of their love. Most of these offerings and acknowledgments, without doubt, would be merely ceremonial. Yet the young King's delight in his visit had been genuine, and his frank enjoyment of all Venice offered had won him her sympathy and even her affection. Memories of the freedom of his stay went with him to the routine of his kingship, and he looked backwards with delight to her winged pleasures. She had spread gifts out before him, as she does before all, but in his own hands he had carried the key of her inmost treasures; for his spirit was joyful and joy is the key to the unlocking of her heart.

Chapter Five
A MERCHANT OF VENICE

"SIAMO NOI calcolatori" was the confession of a modern Venetian, quoted lately as expressive of the spirit that governs Venice to-day and has lain at the root of her policy in the past. The confession is striking; for most men, however calculating in practice, acknowledge an ideal of spontaneous generosity which causes them to shun the admission of self-interested motives. The charge, if charge it can be termed, is an old one. Again and again it has been brought against Venice by those to whom her greatness has been a stumbling-block—"sono calcolatori." But perhaps if the indictment be rightly understood it will be found to need, not so much a denial as an extension, a fuller statement of meaning. And this Professor Molmenti has supplied in his *Venice in the Middle Ages*.1 "The Venetians," he says, in commenting on the support they lent to the Crusades, "never forgot their commercial and political interests in their zeal for the faith; they intended to secure for themselves a market in every corner of the globe. But their so-called egoism displayed itself in a profound attachment to their country and their race; and these greedy hucksters, these selfish adventurers, as they are sometimes unjustly called, had at bottom a genuine belief in objects high and serious; the merchant not seldom became a hero. These lords of the sea knew how to wed the passion of Christianity to commercial enterprise, and welded the aspirations of the faith with the interests of their country, proving by their action not only how vain and sterile is an idealism which consumes itself in morbid dreams, but also that the mere production of riches will lead to ruin unless it be tempered, legalised, almost, we would say, sanctified, by the serene and lifegiving breath of the ideal." But because she was supremely successful in her undertakings, Venice won for herself much perplexed and hostile comment from those who were jealous of a mastery sustained with such apparently effortless self-possession—of an organisation so complete, so silent, so pervasive. She has been accused of perfidy, of cruelty, in short, of shameless egoism. A nation, a state, is pledged to the preservation of its identity, its conceptions must be bounded and constantly measured by the power of other states. The neighbours of Venice in the days of her glory were selfish and calculating also; her prominence was due not so much to special weapons as to her skill in wielding weapons everywhere in use.

1 Translated by Mr. Horatio Browne.

And what can we say of the ends to which she directed her success, the scope of her arts, the nature of her pleasures? It must be admitted by all that the soul of Venice was capacious, unique in its harmony of imagination and political acumen; unique in its power of commanding and retaining respect. A great soul was in the men of Venice; it was present in all their activities, in their commerce as in their art. The two were most intimately allied. Again and again the chroniclers of Venice crown their catalogue of her glories with the reminder that their foundation is in commerce, that the Venetians are a nation of shopkeepers, and "you have only come to such estate by reason of the trade done by your shipping in various parts of the world." Even in the fifteenth century it was deemed complimentary to say to a newly elected Doge, "You have been a great trader in your young days." The greatness of Venice was coincident with the greatness of her trade. She was lit, it is true, with the ancient stars of her splendour after the mortal blow had been struck at her commerce by the discovery of the Cape route to the East, but the old unity of her strength had been lost—the firm foundations of the days when the nobles of Venice had been the directors of her enterprise. And at the end of the fifteenth century they no longer sat, in their togas, behind the counters in Rialto, or made the basements of their houses into stores. They had ceased to apprentice their sons to the merchants on the sea-going galleys. They still acted as commanders of the ships in times of war, but in intervals of peace the gulf between noble and merchant was constantly being enlarged. The commercial traveller was no longer considered one of the most distinguished of citizens. The corner stone had been taken from the building of Rialto; it had begun to crumble to the dissolution lamented by Grevembroch in his strange book on Venetian costumes. In the great days of Venice her commerce was great, and she knew how to robe it in glory, how to attract to it the noblest, and not the meanest, of her sons. Her shops were the objects of her proudest solicitude, and the well-being of her merchants the first of her cares. The hostels provided for foreign traders ranked with the most sumptuous of her palaces, and the rules framed for their guidance were amongst the most liberal in her legislature.

The calculations of Venice, growing with her growth, impressed on her national consciousness the importance of her position midway between the East and the West—her geographical qualification for becoming the mart of the world. With steady and concentrated purpose she devoted her energy to opening up fresh channels of communication. Sometimes by the marriage of a son or daughter of the Doge with the heir of a kingdom or a prince of Constantinople, sometimes by the subjugation of a common foe, Venice wove new threads of intercourse with the East. She always took payment for benefits she conferred in wider trading advantages. Her merchant vessels were not private adventures, they represented state enterprise and were under the control of the central government, travelling with the fleet and capable of reinforcing it at need. Seven merchant convoys left Venice annually for Roumania, Azof, Trebizond, Cyprus, Armenia, France, England, Flanders, Spain, Portugal and Egypt. By means of these vessels the glories of the Orient found their way to the lands of the West; Venice was mistress of the treasures of Arabia, and became their dispenser to Europe. And she was not merely a mart, a counter of interchange; she tested the goods at their source; she was not at the mercy of valuers, her citizen travellers came into touch with the goods on the soil that produced them. The East, to which the art of Venice owes much of its material—its gold, its gems, its colours—was not an unfathomed mine but, in a certain sense, a pleasure-ground for her citizens; they passed to and fro familiarly, guests of its greatest potentates. They stood face to face with Cublay Kaan, the monarch of mystery.

The journeys of the famous Poli are among the most thrilling and significant records of Venetian history. Through them we are able to realise something of the Republic's debt to the lands of the East—a debt not to be summed up in enumeration of embroidery and jewels and perfumes and secrets of colour. In part at least it consisted of legends and traditions that filtered into Venice through the hearing and speech of her travellers— age-old lessons in wisdom, which must have invested some of the common things of Venetian life with new meaning and done something to break down the barriers which ignorance erects between man and man, knowledge and knowledge. In the beautiful Persian rendering of the story of *The Three Magi*, as told by Marco Polo, she came into touch with comparative theology, the familiar Christian tale drawn from an earlier source. Marco Polo tells how he first found at Sara the beautiful tombs of Jaspar, Melchior and Balthasar, with their bodies completely preserved; how the people of that place knew nothing of their history save that they were the bodies of kings; but three days' journey onward he had come to the city of the fire-worshippers and been informed of the three who had set out to worship a newly born Prophet, carrying with them gifts to test the extent of his powers—gold for the earthly King, myrrh for the physician, incense for the God. "And when they were come there where the Child was born, the youngest of these three Kings went all alone to see the Child, and there he found that it was like himself, for it seemed of his age and form. Then he went out much marvelling, and after him went in the second of the Kings, who was near in age to the first, and the Child seemed to him, as to the first, of his own form and age, and he also went out much perplexed. Then went in the third, who was of great age, and it happened to him as to the other two, and he also went out very pensive. And when all the Kings were together, they told one another what they had seen; and they marvelled much and said they would go in all three together. Then they went together into the Child's presence, and they found Him of the likeness and age that He really was, for He was only three days old. Then they adored Him and offered Him their gold and incense and myrrh. The Child took all their offerings and gave them a closed box, and then the three Kings departed and returned to their country." Marco Polo goes on to relate how the Kings, finding the box heavy to bear, sat down by a well to open it, and, when they had opened it, they found only stones inside. These, in their disappointment, they threw into the well and lo! from the stones fire ascended which they gathered up and took home with them to worship. With it they burned all their sacrifices, renewing it from one altar to another. Other tales he told them from the wisdom of the East—of the idealist who found no joy in earthly existence, and the chagrin of his father the King, who surrounded him with luxury and with beautiful maidens, but could not persuade him. One day he rode out on his horse and saw a dead man by the way. And he was filled with horror at a sight which he had never seen before, and he asked those who were with him the meaning of the sight, and they told him it was a dead man. "What," said the son of a King, "then do all men die?" Yes, truly, they say. Then the youth asked no more, but rode on in front in deep thought. And after he had ridden some way he met a very old man who could not walk, and who had no teeth, for he had lost them all by reason of his great age. And when the King's son saw the old man he asked what he was and why he could not walk, and his companions told him that he could not walk from age, and that from age he had lost his teeth. And when the King's son understood about the dead man and the old man, he returned to his palace, and said to himself that he would live no longer in so evil a world, but that he would go "in search of Him who never dies, of Him who made him. And so he departed from his father and from the palace, and went to the mountains, that are very high and impassable, and there he lived all his life, most purely and chastely, and made great abstinence, for certainly if he had been a Christian, he would be a great saint with our Lord Jesus Christ." Did he find his answer in the mountains? Perhaps in some dawn or sunset he learned of the nature of "Him who made him, of Him who never dies"; perhaps among the wild creatures he learned before he was old to sing the lauds of our sister Death. But Polo's comment on the story is interesting, for the Venetians would have little natural sympathy with its hero. They would prefer Carpaccio's fairy prince who forsook his kingdom to follow Ursula and her virgins. The tale of one who dared not look on life in company with his kind, would strike a chill across the full-blooded natures of Venice, so eager to grasp at all that ministered to enjoyment and vitality.

SAN GIORGIO.

But Marco's pack held stories of a more tangible kind—tales of the Palace of Cublay Kaan, with its hall that held six thousand men, the inside walls covered with gold and silver and pictures of great beasts, and the outside rainbow-coloured, shining like crystal in the sun, and a landmark far and wide. And within the circuit of the palace walls was a green pleasure mound covered with trees from all parts and with a green palace on its summit. "And I tell you that the mound and the trees and the palace are so fair to see that all who see them have joy and gladness, and therefore has the great Sire had them made, to have that beautiful view and to receive from it joy and solace." He tells of the wonderful Zecca where coins of the Great Kaan are stamped—not made of metal, but of black paper—which may be refused nowhere throughout the Kaan's dominions on pain of death. All who are possessed of gold and treasure are obliged to bring goods several times in the year, and receive coins of bark in exchange; and therefore, Marco explains, "is Cublay richer than all else in the world." He describes the posting system, the rich palaces built for the housing of messengers, the trees planted along the merchant routes to act as signposts on the road; "for," he says, "you will find these trees along the desert way, and they are a great comfort to merchant and messenger." Visitors to the chapel of San Giorgio dei Schiavoni will recall the use that Carpaccio has made of these palm-tree signposts in the *Death of St. Jerome* and the *Victory of St. George*. Marco tells of magnificent feasts made by the Great Kaan on his birthday and on New Year's Day. He delights in stories of the chase within the domain of Cublay's palace of Chandu (perhaps the Xanadu of Coleridge) the walls of which enclosed a sixteen-mile circuit, with fountains and rivers and lawns and beasts of every kind. He describes in detail, as of special interest to his hearers, the size and construction of the rods of which the Palace of Canes was built and the two hundred silken cords with which it was secured during the summer months of its existence. He speaks of the "weather magic" by which rain and fog are warded off from this palace; and of the Great Kaan's fancy that the blood of a royal line should not be spilt upon the ground to be seen of sun and air, and of his consequent device for the murder of his uncle Nayan, whom he tossed to death in a carpet. Baudas (Baghdad), he says, is the chief city of the Saracens. A great river flows through it to the Indian Ocean, which may be reached in eighteen days. The city is full of merchants and of traffic; it produces *nasich* and *nac* and *cramoisy*, and gold and silver brocades richly embroidered with design of birds and of beasts; and the woods of Bastra, between Baudas and the sea, produce the finest dates in the world. He recounts the taking of this Baudas in the year 1 by Alaü, the Great Kaan's brother, who, when he had taken it, discovered therein a tower belonging to the Caliph full of gold and silver and other treasure, so that there never was so much seen at one time in one place. When Alaü beheld the great heap of treasure, he was amazed and sent for the Caliph into his presence and asked him why he had amassed so great a treasure and what he had intended to do with it. "Did you not know that I was your enemy and coming to lay you waste?" he demanded. "Why, therefore, did you not take your treasure and give it to knights and soldiers to defend you and your city?" The caliph replied nothing, for he did not know what to answer. So Alaü continued, "Caliph, I see you love your treasure so much, I will give you this treasure of yours to eat." So he had the Caliph shut up in the tower and commanded that nothing should be given him to eat or drink, saying, "Caliph, eat now as much treasure as you will, for you shall never eat or drink anything else." And he left the Caliph in the tower, where, at the end of four days, he died. Marco must have opened up to his listeners in Venice horizons of lands almost comparable in extent to the sea-spaces familiar to their thoughts from infancy. He spoke of deserts of many days' journey, of the port of Hormos at the edge of one of the most beautiful of the plains—a city whence precious stones and spices and cloths of silver and gold brought by the merchants from India were shipped to all parts of the world.

But the Poli brought more tangible trophies than the most circumstantial of tales in their pack. Foolish artists might have held themselves rich with these, but the honour of their family would demand better credentials before welcoming fantastically arrayed strangers into its bosom. The courtyard of the house behind the Malibran, at which on their return from their travels they demanded admission, is known still as the Corte del Milione, and its walls are still enriched with Byzantine cornice and moulding, and with sculptured beasts as strange as any to be met with in Cublay's preserves. The three travellers had the appearance of Tartars, and from long disuse of their language they spoke in broken Italian. Tradition tells of the way in which they heaped exploit upon exploit in the attempt to convince their incredulous relatives of their identity; and at last, according to Ramusio, they invited a number of their relations to a superb banquet, at which they themselves appeared in long robes of crimson satin. When the guests were set down, these robes were torn into strips and distributed amongst the servants. Through various metamorphoses of damask and velvet they came at last to the common dresses in which they had arrived. And when the tables were moved and the servants had gone, Marco, as being the youngest, began to rip up the seams and welts of these costumes and take out from them handfuls of rubies and sapphires, carbuncles, diamonds and emeralds. There was no longer any doubt or delay; the shaggy tartar beards had lost all their terrors. These men, who had suddenly displayed "infinite riches in a little room," must undoubtedly be what they claimed to be; happy the family to which the magicians belonged; the Doge's Palace need not be afraid to welcome them; they must be set high in the State.

Yet the accumulation of treasure was by no means the most noteworthy act of their drama. The Poli had been more than mere traders; from the first they had been diplomatists of a high order. Their career seems to give us the key to some of the wonderful faces that appear in the crowds pictured by Venetian painters, especially those of Carpaccio. They are the faces of men who have met the crisis of life unalarmed, by virtue of a combination of daring and wisdom which is no common possession. They are not cold; if they are severe they are full of feeling—sensitive to the pathos and humour as well as the sternness of reality. The Poli had been obliged to furnish themselves with patience in lands where the transit of a plain is measured in weeks; three years' residence in a city of Persia is mentioned as a matter of detail. We are not told the reason of delay, only that they could not go before or behind. They had travelled in the true spirit of adventure. On that first journey, when Marco was not of the company, the Great Kaan's messengers, who came to request an interview for their master, who had never set eyes on a Latin, had found the two brothers open-minded and trustful. They had acquitted themselves well in Cublay's presence, answering all his questions wisely and in order. He had inquired as to the manners and customs of Europe, and particularly as to Western methods of government and the Christian Church and its Head. He had been "glad beyond measure" at what he had heard of the deeds of the Latins, and decided to send a request to the Christian Apostle for one hundred men learned in the Christian law and the Seven Arts and capable of teaching his people that their household gods were works of the devil and why the faith of the West was better than theirs. The thought of the lamp burning before the sepulchre of God in Jerusalem had stirred his imagination, and he craved some of its oil for the light of his temple, or, maybe, his pleasure dome. So the two Venetians had set out for Europe on his strange embassy. They were provided with a golden tablet on which the Kaan had inscribed orders for the supplying of their needs, food, horses, escorts in all the countries through which they should pass. At the end of three years, after long delays on account of the snows, they arrived at the port of Layas in Armenia, and from Layas they had come to Acre in April of the year 1. At Acre they had found that Pope Clement IV was dead, and no new election had as yet been made. Venetian history teems with dramatic situations, but it would be difficult to find any stranger than that in which the Polo brothers now found themselves placed. Merchants of Venice, they came as ambassadors from the Lord of All the Tartars to demand missionaries from the Father of Christendom, who was not able to supply them because he was not in existence. In their dilemma at Acre they consulted Theobald of Piacenza, Legate of Egypt, who advised them to await the new Pope's election and meanwhile to return to their homes. His advice was accepted, and the two brothers made their way onwards to Venice, where one of them, Nicolas, discovered his son, young Marco, a lad of fifteen years old. They remained in Venice for two years, but when, at the end of that time, no Pope had yet been elected, the brothers felt their return to the Kaan could be deferred no longer. There is something touching in their fidelity to the pledge they had given and the constancy of their merchant faith. They prepared to set out again. This time little Marco went with them on an absence that lasted for seventeen years, and was to gather a greater treasure for the world than any diamonds and rubies and velvets to be prodigally scattered on the floor of the Corte del Milione. At Acre they obtained Theobald's permission to fetch some of the holy oil desired by the Kaan from Jerusalem. The journey to Jerusalem performed, they returned once more to Acre, and finally set forth on their return journey to the Kaan with a letter from Theobald testifying that they had done all in their power, "but since there was no Apostle, they could not carry the embassy." But when they had gone as far on their journey as Layas, they were followed by letters from Theobald, who was now Pope Gregory of Piacenza, begging their return. They complied with great joy and set sail for Acre in a galley provided for their use by the King of Armenia. This was the hour of their triumph, for they were received by the Pope with great honour, given costly presents for the Kaan, and provided with two friars of very great learning. The names of these two are possibly better withheld, for they were more learned than courageous. When they had come as far on their journey as Layas, their incipient fears of the land of the Tartars were wrought to a pitch by the sight of the Saracen Army which was being brought against Armenia by the Sultan of Babylon, and they insisted on handing their credentials over to the Poli and returning at once to Italy. And the brothers were forced to go on their way with worse than no preachers of their faith, with tidings of their defection.

For three and a half years they journeyed on, detained often by floods and bad weather. The news of their coming travelled before them to the Kaan, and he sent his servants forty days' journey to meet them. The Kaan received them with joy, was graciously pleased with the letters and credentials sent by the Pope, and accepted young Marco as his liegeman and responsible messenger. Marco sped well in learning the language, customs and writing of the Tartars, but it is clear he must have acquired other than scholastic accomplishments. He was endowed with tact and power of observation, and returned from his first embassy full of news of the men and customs he had encountered; "for he had seen on several occasions that when the messengers the Great Kaan had sent into various parts of the world returned and told him the results of the embassy on which they had gone, and could tell him no other news of the countries where they had been, the Kaan said they were ignorant fools." For seventeen years young Messer Marco was employed in continual coming and going. He was learned in many strange and hidden things, and was placed in honour high above the barons—the darling of Cublay's heart. Again and again the three Venetians asked for leave of absence to visit their country, but so great was the love Cublay bore to them that he could not bear to be parted from them; until at last an embassy arrived from Argon, King of Levant, asking for a new wife of the lineage of his dead wife Bolgana, and the Kaan is persuaded by Argon's messengers to allow Marco and his two uncles to depart with them in charge of the lady. They set out by sea, and after some twenty months' sailing and many disasters arrived at their destination. King Argon was dead, and the lady Cocachin was bestowed on his son. Of the six hundred followers who had set out with them on their journey only eighteen had survived it. Their mission accomplished, the Poli made their way to Trebizond, from Trebizond to Constantinople and from Constantinople to Venice. This was in the year 1.

THE DOGANA.

And how would Venice, the place of his birth, reveal herself to Marco, now he had seen so many wonders and glories in distant lands? We may imagine the sun to have been setting as the travellers turned into the Lido port, dropping a globe of molten fire vast and mysterious through the haze, while the last dim rays gleamed golden on the windows of the Riva degli Schiavoni. Venice lay among her waters, blue and glittering, interspersed with jewelled marsh. The last gulls of those that so gallantly had dipped and sailed all day upon the water were flying home, their breasts and wings radiant in the level sunlight round the home-coming ship. Many citizens of Venice must have been at the Lido port, thronging to meet the merchant vessels, to greet their friends or to have news of them from others. But none came to meet these three travellers; alone they embarked in a gondola bearing their cargo with them. Venice had clothed herself in all her beauty to give them welcome. Which of Cublay's glories could rival this splendour of the lagoon with its countless treasures of light? The marsh lay in unequal patches, each outlined with a luminous silver rim—a magic carpet of dusky olive, threaded with strands of radiant azure and sprinkled with ruby and amethyst. As their gondola moved slowly down towards the city, the boats of the night fishers passed with the silence of shadows between them and the glow. And when here and there a fisher alighted on the marsh or moved across it like a spirit stepping on the waters, he must have seemed to Marco the very memory and renewal of those strange Eastern stories of which his mind was full. So, under the mystic glow of the desert, he had seen figures of the caravan rise and move against the tinted haze of the oasis. Onwards glided the boat towards the Basin of San Marco— westward the luminous wonder of lagoon and marsh, and a cold, clear intensity of stirring water to the east. And as they drew nearer and ever nearer, our travellers' hearts beat high with the wonders of the city of their birth. The stars were piercing the night sky in countless numbers: the yellow lights of the city quivered along the Riva: the masts of the fishing-fleet swung clear against the pale western glow in the waterway of the Giudecca: the flowing tide wound silver coils about the black shadows of their hulls. Past the Dogana, keystone of Venice to the Eastern traveller, their little boat moved down the quiet waters of the Grand Canal, deep into the heart of that great shadowy city, apparent Queen over all the glories of the Cities of the East.

Chapter Six
VENICE OF CRUSADE AND PILGRIMAGE

THE story of Venice and the Crusades forms one of the most interesting pages of her history in relation to the East. The gradual awakening of her consciousness to the fact that the pilgrimages to the Holy Land might be of close significance to herself culminates in her attitude towards the great Fourth Crusade at the opening of the thirteenth century. The Crusades were, in fact, a commercial speculation for Venice, but a speculation into which she infused all the vitality and fulness of her nature. And she became, not merely a place of passage for the East, but a superb depository of relics to detain pilgrims on their outward way; a hostel so royally fitted with food for their senses, their religious cravings and their mystic imaginings, that one and another may well have been beguiled into delaying their departure for more strenuous sanctities. The narratives of the pilgrims, with their enthusiasms, their details of relics, their records of Venetian ceremonies, religious, commercial or domestic, coloured by their quaintly intimate personal impressions, form one of the most picturesque pages of Venetian chronicle.

Pietro Casola, a Milanese pilgrim of the late fifteenth century, gives us a picture of a city that is sumptuous and rich in all its dealings, yet pervaded by a harmony and decorum that has stamped itself on the face of each individual citizen. We feel that Pietro Casola has really had a vision of the meaning of Venice, when, among the inventory of wonders of the Mass for the pilgrims on Corpus Christi day, of the velvets, crimson and damask and scarlet, the cloth of gold and togas sweeping the ground, each finer than the last, he pauses to add, "There was great silence, greater than is ever observed at such festivals, even in the gathering of so many Venetian gentlemen, so that you could hear everything. And it seemed to me that everything was ruled by one alone, who was obeyed by each man without resistance. And at this I wondered greatly, for never had I seen so great obedience at such spectacles." In the record of this arresting impression, more even than in the description of many coloured drapery and white cloths spread on the piazza, of the groves of oak-trees bordering the route of the procession and the candles lit among them, we seem to see before us the rhythmic solemnity of that unique *Procession* on the Piazza of Gentile Bellini. We need only Casola's other observant characterisation of the Venetian gentleman to complete the picture. "I have considered," he says, "the quality of these Venetian gentlemen, who for the most part are fair men and tall, astute and most subtle in their dealings; and you must needs, if you would treat with them, keep your eyes and ears open. They are proud; I think it is on account of their great rule. And when a son is born to a Venetian, they say among themselves, 'A Signor is born into the world.' In their way of living at home they are sparing and very modest; outside they are very liberal. The city of Venice retains its old manner of dress, and they never change it; that is to say, they wear a long garment of whatever colour they choose. No one ever goes out by day without his toga, and for the most part a black one, and they have carried this custom to such a point that all nations of the world who are lodging here in Venice, from the greatest to the least, observe this style, beginning from the gentlemen to the mariners and galleymen; a dress certainly full of confidence and gravity. They look like doctors of law, and if any were to appear outside his house without his toga he would be thought a fool." Without doors the women also belonged to this sober company, or at least the marriageable maidens and those who were no longer of the number of the "belle giovani"; so sombrely were they covered when outside their houses, and especially in church, that Casola says he at first mistook them all for widows, or nuns of the Benedictine Order. But for the "belle giovani" it is another matter; they give relief to the week-day sobriety of these Venetians, so decorous and black when off duty, though revelling in such richness of velvet and brocade when the trumpet of a public function stirs their blood.

THE SHADOW OF THE CAMPANILE.

We are indebted to Casola for a picture of a Venetian domestic festival at the birth of a child to the Delfini family. He realised fully that he was admitted, together with the orator of the King of France, in order that he might act as reporter of Venetian magnificence. It was in a room "whose chimney-piece was all of Carrara marble shining as gold, so subtly worked with figures and leaves, that Praxiteles and Pheidias could not have exceeded it. The ceiling of the room was so finely decorated with gold and ultramarine, and the walls so richly worked, that I cannot make report of it. One desk alone was valued at five hundred ducats, and the fixtures of the room were in the Venetian style, such beautiful and natural figures, so much gold everywhere, that I know not if in the time of Solomon, who was King of the Jews, when silver was reputed more vile than carrion, there was such abundance as was here seen. Of the ornaments of the bed and of the lady ... I have thought best rather to keep silence than to speak for fear I should not be believed. Another thing I will speak the truth about, and perhaps I shall not be believed—a matter in which the ducal orator would not let me lie. There were in the said room twenty-five Venetian damsels, each one fairer than the last, who were come to visit the lady who had borne a child. Their dress was most discreet, as I said above, *alla veneziana*: they showed no more than four to six finger breadths of bare neck below their shoulders back and front. These damsels had so many jewels on their heads and round their necks and on their hands—namely, gold, precious stones and pearls—that it was the opinion of those who were there that they were worth a hundred thousand ducats. Their faces were superbly painted, and so also the rest of them that was bare." The account of this sumptuous interior is peculiarly valuable when we realise the date to which it belongs, the period of the first greatness of Venetian Art, a period which has been sometimes regarded as one of almost naïve simplicity. Casola, with his customary exactitude, dwells on the frugality of Venetian gentlemen in the matter of food—a frugality that caused the guest to reflect that the Venetians cared more to feed the eye than the palate. It was not yet the period of the sumptuous living deplored by Calmo only half a century later.

Casola was a more secularly minded pilgrim than the priest of Florence, Ser Michele, who paid five visits to the bones of the Holy Innocents at Murano, and only at the fifth visit was counted worthy, as he humbly deemed, to see the relics: Providence, in the form of the sacristan, having till then failed him. The more festive Casola—who paid repeated visits to Rialto, "which seemed to be the source of all the gardens in the world," who spent one day in vain attempts to count the multitudinous boats in and about the city, and who was so frivolous, for all his long white beard, as to buy a false front on the piazza—in the midst of his expatiations on the Venetian maidens, pulls himself suddenly together with a sense of incongruity between his diversions and his goal, and shakes himself free from the allurements of Venice, crying: "But I am a priest, in the way of the saints; I did not try to look into their lives any further. To me it seemed better, as I have said above, to go in search of the churches and monasteries and to see the relics of which there are so many. And this seemed to me a good work for a pilgrim who was awaiting the departure of the vessel to go to the Holy Sepulchre, bringing the time to an end as well as he could." In the Accademia at Venice there is a curious little painting, attributed to Carpaccio, of the assembly of the martyrs of Mount Ararat in the Church of Sant' Antonio di Castello, which stood once on the site of the Public Gardens. It was a familiar sight for Venice, the dedication of pilgrims that is represented here; and there is a strange pathos in the slim, small figures as they move in two lines half-wavering up the aisle, each wearing a crown of thorns, perhaps in prophecy of coming martyrdom. They are not marching confidently to victory like an army; their crosses are held at all angles, forming errant patterns among themselves. Some are girt for their journey in short vestments under their long robes. It is curiously unlike a procession native to the city; there is a dreamlike, mystic quality about it and a lack of body in its motion which is enhanced, perhaps, by the extreme detail with which the interior of the church is transcribed—the models of vessels in the rafters; the votive limbs and bones hung on the wooden screen, offerings of the diseased cured by miracle, as they may be seen in San Giovanni e Paolo to-day; the coiled rope of the lamp-pulley; the board with a church notice printed on it; and everywhere, winding in and out of the picture, seen through the portal of entrance, disappearing behind the sanctuary screen, the interminable procession of the ten thousand little pilgrims.

In 1198 the lords of France flocked with enthusiasm to a crusade preached by Foulques de Nuilly under the authority of Innocent III. After much discussion of practical ways and means, with which they were less amply provided than with spiritual enthusiasm, they made choice of six ambassadors who should procure the necessities of the enterprise, Jofroi de Villeharduin, Mareschal of Champagne, Miles li Brabant, Coëns de Bethune, Alars Magnarians, Jean de Friaise, and Gautiers de Gaudonville. Venice was decided on by them as the State most likely to provide what they stood in need of—ships for the journey—and they departed to sound the mind of the Republic, arriving in the first week of Lent in the year 1. Venice, in the person of the Doge, Henry Dandolo, opened the negotiations; the messengers were made to feel it was no light thing they asked. They were received and lodged with highest honour, but they were made to wait for a Council to assemble, which should consider the matter of their request. After some days they were admitted to the Ducal Palace to deliver their message; and its purport was this: "Sir, we are come to you from the high barons of France who have taken the sign of the Cross to avenge the shame of Jesus Christ, and to conquer Jerusalem if God will grant it them; and because they know that no people have such power as you and your people, they pray you for God's sake to have pity on the land over seas and the avenging of the shame of Jesus Christ, so that they may have ships and the other things necessary." The spiritual and sentimental appeal is left unanswered by the Doge. He asks simply, "In what way?" "In all ways," say the messengers, "that you recommend or advise, which they would be able to fulfil." Again the Doge expresses wonder at the magnitude of what they ask, bidding them not marvel if another eight days' waiting is required of them before the final answer can be given. At the date fixed by the Doge they returned to the Palace. Villeharduin excuses himself from telling all the words that were said and unsaid, but the gist of the Doge's offer was this, that it depended on the consent of the Great Council and the rest of the Republic. Venice should provide vessels of transport for four thousand five hundred horses and squires and twenty thousand foot soldiers, and viands to last the whole company nine months. The agreement was to hold good for a year from the time of starting, and the sum total of the provision was to be eighty-five thousand marks. But Venice would go further, for the love of God, and launch fifty galleys at her own expense on condition of receiving the half of all the conquests that were made by land and sea. Nothing remained but to win the consent of the Great Council and ask a formal ratification from the people. Full ten thousand persons assemble in "the chapel of San Marco, the fairest that ever was," and the Doge recommends them to hear the Mass, and to pray God's counsel concerning the request of the envoys. It will be seen that all is practically accomplished before the question is put to the people or God's grace asked on the undertaking, but no item of the formality is omitted. The envoys are sent for by the Doge that they may themselves repeat their request humbly before the people, and they came into the church "much stared at by the crowd who had never seen them." Again the appeal is made, Jofroi de Villeharduin taking up the word by the agreement and desire of the other envoys. We can picture the strange thrill that ran through the great multitude as that single voice broke the silence of St. Mark's with its burden of passionate tribute to the greatness of Venice: "'Therefore have they chosen you because they know that no people accustomed to going on the seas have such power as you and your people; and they commanded us to throw ourselves at your feet and not to rise until you had consented to have pity on the Holy Land beyond the seas.' Now the six messengers knelt, weeping bitterly, and the Doge and all the others cried out with one voice and raised their hands on high and said, 'We grant it, we grant it.' And the noise and tumult and lament of it were so great that never had any man known a greater." Then the Doge himself mounted the lectern and put before the people the meaning of the alliance that had been sought with them in preference to all other peoples by "the best men of the world." "I cannot tell you," says Villeharduin, "all the good and fair words that the Doge spoke. At last the matter was ended, and the following day the charters were drawn up and made and sealed."

THE CLOCK TOWER FROM GALLERY OF SAN
MARCO.

The time of gathering for the pilgrims was fixed for the
following year 1, at the feast of St. John, and amid many tears
of piety and devotion the Doge and deputies swore to abide by
their charters, and the envoys of both parties set out for Rome
to receive the confirmation of their covenant from Innocent
III. But the drama which had begun amid such moving
demonstrations of good will and Christian sentiment
necessarily had its dilemmas and its complications. It was
essential to the fulfilling of the pact that all the crusaders
should assemble at Venice to pay their toll, and embark on the
ships; otherwise the crusaders could not hope to provide the
money due to the Venetians. The Republic, for its part, had
amply fulfilled its compact. All who arrived were received with
joy and lodged most honourably at San Nicolo del Lido. The

chronicle can find no parallel for the richness of the provision made for the would-be crusaders. But there were, alas, three times as many vessels as there were men and horses to fill them.—"Ha! it was a great shame," bursts out Villeharduin, "that the rest who went to the other ports did not come here." The dilemma was a serious one. Even of those who were there, some declared themselves unable to pay their passage, and the money could in no way be made up. Some were for sacrificing their whole estate that the Venetians should not lose by the defection of the others, but the counsel found small support among those who now wished to be rid of their bargain. But the small party who felt themselves, in a sense, the conscience of the Crusade carried the day. "Rather will we give all we possess and go poor among the host, than that it should disperse and come to naught; for God will render it to us at His good pleasure." So the Counts of Flanders, Loys, Hues de St. Pol and their party began to collect together all their goods and all they could borrow. "Then you might have seen a vast quantity of gold and silver borne to the palace of the Doge to make payment. And when they had paid, there still was lacking from the covenant thirty-four thousand marks of silver. And those who had kept back what they possessed and would give nothing were very glad at this, for by this means they thought the expedition would have failed. But God who counsels the disconsolate would not so suffer it." The Doge put before his people that not only would their just claim remain unsatisfied though they should exact from the crusaders the utmost they could collect, but they would bring discredit on themselves by acting as strict justice would permit. He suggested the combining of two advantages, a material and moral. Let them, he suggests, demand the reconquest of Zara as substitute for the debt, that they may not only have the fame of possessing the city but the praise of generosity. And Dandolo, the old wise doughty Doge, has yet another suggestion to propose. There was a great festival one Sunday in San Marco, and the citizens and barons and pilgrims were assembled before High Mass began. Then amid the silent expectation of the great gathering the Doge mounted the lectern and made the famous offer of his own person as leader of the host. "'I am an old man,' he said, 'and feeble, and should be feeling need of repose, for I am infirm in body. But I see there is none who could so well rule and lead you as I who am your lord. If you will consent that I take the sign of the Cross to preserve and guide you, and that my son remain in my stead and keep the city, I would gladly go to live and die with you and with the pilgrims.' And when they heard, they cried all with one voice: 'We pray you for God's sake to grant us this, and to do so and to come with us.' And the people of the city and the pilgrims, felt deep compassion at this, and they wept many tears, thinking how that valiant man had so much need to stay behind, for he was an old man, and though his eyes were still fair to look on he could not see with them on account of a wound which he had received in his head. Nevertheless he had a great heart. Ha! how little they resembled him who had gone to other ports to avoid danger! So he came from the pulpit and went to the altar and knelt down, weeping bitterly, and they sewed the cross for him on a great cotton cap because he desired that the people might see it. And the Venetians began to take the cross in great numbers, and many on that very day, and still the number of crusaders was few enough." It was no wonder that the pilgrims had great joy in the crusaders for the good will and valour they felt to be in them. Whatever aim may previously have been uppermost as an incentive to enthusiasm and self-oblation, there was no doubt that Venice now was giving of her best. This retiring of the old Doge from his ducal throne to embark on a more arduous leadership is one of the most moving episodes in the annals San Marco.

But at this moment an event occurred that changed, or rather diverted into a new channel the current of the Crusade, providing in fact, as our chronicler Villeharduin remarks, the true occasion of his book. Into the midst of the pilgrims assembled at Verona on their way to Venice there came Alexius, son of Isaac the deposed Emperor of Constantinople, in quest of help against his usurping uncle. What more opportune than the neighbouring host of "the most valiant men on earth" for aiding in the recovery of his lost kingdom and the reinstatement of his tortured father. To the crusaders, and especially we may believe, to the Venetians, this new motive did not come amiss. It is startlingly like life, this Fourth Crusade, with its original aim thus gradually becoming but a secondary purpose in a far more complicated scheme, a middle distance in an increasingly extended horizon. The relief of the Holy Sepulchre, the avenging of the shame of Christ, assume in fact a rather shadowy outline in a prospect dominated by Zara and Constantinople.

The departure from Venice did not mark the term of the obstructions to which the Crusade was fated. The disgraceful contest between the French and the Venetians within the streets of Zara, the defection of a number of the pilgrims, the death of others at the hands of the wild inland inhabitants of Dalmatia—all these causes reduced the already meagre company before it had well started on its way. The Pope was placed in the dilemma of strongly disapproving the secular turn given to the Crusade, while realising that the Venetian fleet was the only means for accomplishing his ends in Palestine. His solution was to absolve the barons for the siege of Zara, permitting them still to use the fleet—though the devil's instrument—while Venice, the provider, remained under interdict. We here come into contact with an element of singular interest in the relations of Venice and the East—her attitude towards the Papacy. The independence of San Marco was one of the essential articles of the Venetian creed. In spiritual matters none could more devoutly bow to the Apostle of Christendom; but the spiritual supremacy was an inland sea to Venice: it must be stable, fixed, defined; it must not flow with a tide upon the temporal shores where her heart and treasure lay. The authority of San Marco was a political principle. All state ceremonies were bound up with San Marco; the Ducal Palace itself was subsidiary to the Palace of St. Mark. How should a State that had sheltered, traditionally at least, a Pope "stando occulto propter timorem" that had acted as mediator between Pope and Emperor and seen the Emperor's head bowed to the ground on the pavement of San Marco— how should such a State be subordinate to any rule but its own complete self-consciousness? Venice always followed the eminently practical rule of allowing much freedom in non-essentials in order to preserve more closely her control over the really material issues. The attitude always maintained by her with regard to the Inquisition is so closely parallel to her relations with the East and the pagans of the East, constantly deprecated by the Pope, that we may fitly quote here Paolo Sarpi's admirable reply to the papal protests against conferring the doctorate in Padua on Protestants; the principle is the same, though limited in that instance to a particular and seemingly divergent issue. "If anyone openly declared his intention of conferring the doctorate on heretics, or admitted anyone to it who openly and with scandal professed himself to be such, it might be said that he had failed to persecute heresy;

but, it being the opinion of the most Serene Republic that heretics and those who are known for such should not be admitted to the doctorate, and it being our duty to consider Catholic anyone who does not profess the contrary, no smallest scandal can accrue to the religion even though it should chance that one not known for such were to receive the doctorate. The doctorate in philosophy and medicine is a testimonial that the scholar is a good philosopher and physician and that he may be admitted to the practise of that art, and to say that a heretic is a good doctor does not prejudice the Catholic faith; certainly it would prejudice it if anyone were to say that such a man was a good theologian." This was the position of Venice with regard to her pagan allies, the meaning of her superbly fitted lodges for Turk, infidel and heretic. The Saracen, the Turk and the Infidel might not be a good theologian, but he was a good trader, a channel for the glories with which Venice loved to clothe and crown herself. He was a part of her life more essentially and more irrevocably than the prelates of holy Church; his ban would have been more terrible to Venice than papal thunders. It was not primarily as hot sons of the Church, consumed with fire for the shame of the Holy Sepulchre that the Venetians with such generous provision prepared their ships for the Crusade: it was as men of business with no small strain of fire in their blood and a high sense of the glorious worth and destiny of their city.

THE HORSES OF SAN MARCO, LOOKING SOUTH.

There were moments of inspiration for the Crusaders amid all their toils and internal strife, and not least was the first view of Constantinople which had been for so long the emporium of Venice. The fleet had harboured at the abbey of St. Etienne, three miles from Constantinople, and Villeharduin describes the wonder and enthusiasm of those who saw then for the first time the marvellous city "that was sovereign over all others," with its rich towers and palaces and churches and high encircling walls. "And you must know there was no heart there so daring but trembled." We are reminded of this picture of Constantinople when we stand face to face with Carpaccio's city in the *Combat of St. George*. It so successfully combines solidity and strength with the airy joy of watch-towers and towers of pleasure, that at first we have only the impression of fantastic play of architecture; but by degrees we come to feel the seacoast country of Carpaccio, that at first seemed so wild and unmanned, to be in fact bristling with defence and preparation. It is immensely strong in fortifications, no dream or fairy citadel. It is begirt with towers and walls along the water; strongholds lurk among the loftiest crags; towers of defence and battlements peer over the steep hillside; and, if we look closer, we see the towers are thronged with men. We remember Villeharduin's note, "There were so many men on the walls and on the towers that it seemed as if they were made of nothing but people." It is a sumptuous city, too, that we see in glimpses through the gateway, the city of a great oriental potentate.

We cannot follow Villeharduin through the vicissitudes of the siege and counter-siege. He himself confesses in the relation of one point alone that sixty books would not be able to recount all the words that were spoken, and the counsels that were given and taken. In the simple, terse and trenchant style that Frenchmen, and especially the Frenchmen of the old chronicles, know how to wield so perfectly, he tells us of the Doge's wise counsel that the city should be approached by way of the surrounding islands whence they might gather stores; of the lords' neglect of this counsel, "just as if no one of them had ever heard of it"; of their investment of the palace of Alexius in the place named Chalcedony, that was "furnished with all the delights of the human body that could be imagined befitting the dwelling of a prince"; of the capture of the city and the ravishing of its treasures that were so great "that no man could come to an end of counting the silver and the gold and plate and precious stones and samite and silken cloth and dresses *vaire* and grey, and ermines and all precious things that were ever found on earth. And Jofroi de Villcharduin, the Marshall of Champagne, will bear good witness that to his knowledge since the centuries began there was never so great gain in a single city." The division of the booty necessarily occasioned heart-burning and revealed certain vices of "covetoise" undreamed before. And as time went on and still the passage to Palestine was delayed the sanctuaries of the Greek Church were treated with barbarous irreverence and despoiled of their treasure and sacred vessels. Then with the retaking of Constantinople from Marzuflo there followed a time of abandonment of men and leaders to their fiercest passions and the almost total destruction of the city. Here again Venice stepped in, as the merchant had stepped in to rescue treasure from the pile of Savonarola, to enrich herself from the ruins of Constantinople.

The taking of Constantinople opened another door into the Eastern garden from which Venice had already begun to gather so rich an harvest. Picture the freights that Venetian vessels were bearing home in these years of crusade and conquest, to be gathered finally into the garner of St. Mark's! It is strangely thrilling to imagine the first welcome of the four bronze horses, travel-dimmed no doubt, who only found their way to their present station on the forefront of St. Mark's after standing many times in peril of being melted down in the Arsenal where they first were stored. But at last, says Sansovino, their beauty was recognised and they were placed on the church. It is only by degrees that we come to accost and know the exiles one by one. The more outstanding spoils, the Pala d'Oro, the great pillars of Acri, the bronze doors, the horses, the four embracing kings, these are among the first letters of St. Mark's oriental alphabet; but there are many lesser exiles which have found a shelter in the port of Venice, which as we wander among the glorious precincts of San Marco impress themselves upon us one by one; such is the grave-browed, noble head of porphyry that keeps solitary watch towards the waters from the south corner of the outer gallery of San Marco, as if it had been set down a moment by its sculptor and forgotten on the white, marble balustrade. The whole being of San Marco is bound up with the East, and it is another token of the magic of Venice that she has been able to embrace and furnish with a life-giving soil those plants that had been ruthlessly uprooted and had made so long and perilous a journey. The official records, that tell of the arrival from one expedition and another of Eastern vestures for the clothing of San Marco, are not mere inventories to us who have walked upon the variegated pavement between the solemn pillars and seen the sunlight illumine one by one the marbles of the walls, with their imbedded sculpture and mosaic, or gild the depths of the storied cupolas and the luxuriant harmonies of colour and design on the recesses of the windows. They are significant, these records, like the entry in a parish register of the birth of some one whom we love; for the church of San Marco, though in fact a museum of many treasures, is not a museum of foreign treasures. Her spoils are not hung up in her as aliens like the spoils that conquerors bore to ancient temples; they found her a foster-mother of their own blood and kin. She herself is sprung from a plant whose first flowering was not among the floating marshes of the lagoon.

THE HORSES OF SAN MARCO, LOOKING NORTH.

Turn, on a sunny day, from the Molo towards San Marco, passing below the portico of the Ducal Palace adjoining the Piazzetta. Framed by the pointed arch at the end is a portion of the wall which once formed the west tower of the Ducal Palace. This delicate harmony of coloured marbles and sculptured stone seems a rare and beautiful creation, not of stone but of something more plastic, more mobile, so responsive is it to the light, so luminous, so full of feeling. As we draw nearer and it becomes more clearly defined, we see great slabs of marble sawn and spread open like the pages of a book, corresponding in pattern as the veining of a leaf. They are linked by marble rope-work, and between them are inserted smaller slabs of delicately sculptured stone and a wonderful coil of mosaic. It is a veritable patchwork wall, but no less beautiful in its effect of harmony than in its details—the four porphyry figures of embracing kings its corner-stone. This wall is truly a key to the fabric of the church itself; it is like a window into St. Mark's, that treasury of Eastern spoil; the East is in every vein, in every heart-beat of it. The spoil of the temples of ancient gods furnished forth the Church of San Marco as it furnished the saint himself. In this one angle we have cipollino and porphyry, serpentine and verd-antico, marmo greco and eastern mosaic, pillars of granite profound and glittering, breccia africana and paonazetto. The weight of centuries is upon it all; ages of lives have gone to its making, and it came to Venice only when generations had passed over its head. For the human race it has never been but old; the mind loses itself in speculation on that stupendous past that lies between us and the time when stone was not. And yet how strangely through that long, enchanted silence, when the centuries were endowing it with an immensity of strength and hardness and endurance for which we have no word of parallel but in its own nature, it has kept the similitude and mobility of life, at once withholding and revealing the riches of its beauty. How can we wonder that da Contarini, the strange and learned dreamer of the Cinquecento, burst out into a rapture of mystic joy in the presence of San Marco, "that golden church, built by the eternal gods, of our protector, Messer San Marco"? He celebrates the pinnacles and shining columns, the throng of glittering figures that burn like golden spirits in the sunlight, the sculptured marbles polished with soft Ethiopian sand. "It might be said that it has been gathered together from all parts of the world." He then proceeds to seek among the marbles of San Marco those mysterious correspondences which the wonder of men has always felt to exist between human nature and the nature of the stone; he loses himself in contemplation of one after another of the precious marbles that in wide surface or minute mosaic form the priceless garment of St. Mark's temple: diaspro, which must be seen in broad extent to realise its strange radiance, like flocks of cloudlets fleeting before the wind in the full illumination of the setting sun, dazzling our eyes with light; or that other adamantine marble of Africa, the breccia adriana di Tegoli, a harmony of greens before which serpentine and verd-antico must bow; or the most precious porpora of deep and glowing red; or that queen of all the stones, imperial in its beauty, a magnetic stone indeed, drawing the spirit into its luminous depths, weaving round it an enchanted web of secrecy, of divine inter-relations, till the human soul seems to commune with the very soul of colour— *diaspro sanguinoso*. What would not Sir Thomas Browne have read in those eloquent and secret pages where wave follows wave of colour, deep ocean green, pure carmine, translucent amethyst. Diaspro sanguinoso! in the setting of a ring, in the mosaic of a pavement, it is seen a dense green stone spotted with crimson—bloodstone. It is as if you saw the human eye in one of those weird, symbolic paintings of old time, isolated in its socket without the illumination of the human countenance about it. This sanguinary jasper is too subtle, too delicate, too mystical to belong to that titanic family of the stones of Africa. The dreaming soil of Egypt might have given it birth; it might own kinship with the myth of Aurora's kiss; but to us it seems fraught with the magic of a more distant East.

There have been many vindicators of the freedom of Venice; many assertors that, though in appearance subject some time to Byzantium, she has always been politically independent. To us it seems a matter of lesser moment; but whether, in fact or in form, Venice were or were not ever politically dependent on Byzantium, the fact of her artistic dependence is one which she cannot deny without perjuring herself before a thousand witnesses. Document after document more durable than parchment—though many have already perished and many perish daily—attests the debt of Venice to the East. Till she perish altogether at the hands of a relentless, unregarding tyrant—a bastard child of Time misnamed Progress—she must continue to bear witness to her debt. So long as she breathes, each breath confesses it and the East will lay her tribute on the tomb of Venice dead—lamenting as for one of her own children.

Chapter Seven
TWO VENETIAN STATUES

IN two of the public squares of Venice the statues, in bronze, of two of her heroes are set up, the one of a man of war, the other of a comedian: in the Campo di SS. Giovanni e Paolo the statue of Bartolomeo Colleoni, in the Campo di San Bartolomeo that of Carlo Goldoni. The first is a warrior on horseback in full armour, uplifted high above the square, disdaining the companionship of the puny mortals who saunter without a purpose to and fro under his feet. Horse and rider stand self-sufficient and alone; one spirit breathes in both: in the contour of the stern face of the warrior, with its massive chin and proudly disdainful lip, in his throat with the muscles standing out like ropes upon it, and in the sweep of his capacious brow, under which the keenly penetrating eyes hold their object in a grip of iron; and, for the horse, in every line of his superbly curving neck, in the acute serenity of his down-looking eye, and in each curling lock of his mane that seem as if moved together by one controlling impulse. How clear the outline of his skull, everywhere visible beneath its fine covering of flesh and muscle! and his body, like the body of his master, how perfectly responsive an instrument it is! There is nothing here of that wild disorder of the beast untamed, which is mistaken sometimes for strength. The hand of Colleoni is light upon the bridle, the horse glories in a subjection that is itself a triumph: he and his master are one. Do but compare this for a moment with the prodigious mass, the plunging man and beast, that overlook the Riva degli Schiavoni—Victor Emanuel on horseback. It is not altogether an arbitrary contrast; the two great monuments seem to represent Venice before the fall and Venice after. What unity of purpose, what hope of conquest is there in those monstrous figures on the Riva? Beneath this redundancy of flesh and armour how shall they prevail against the world? They are not only different in degree, they are of a different species from Verocchio's horse and rider. The spirit of the first Renaissance is in every line of his great statue—its strength, agility and decorative skill. How studied is the symmetry, the static perfection of the whole! how strongly and yet how delicately he emphasises the rectangular framework of the design! The rod of Colleoni, the trappings of his horse, the tail and legs and body-line—each is made contributive, while the backward poise of the rider balances the forward motion of the horse, and all is thus drawn into the scheme. It is all willed, but with that spontaneity of will which men call inspiration.

This statue, which so marvellously sums up in sculpture the central aim of Venice as a state in the fifteenth century, offers an instructive contrast to that in the Campo di San Bartolomeo, where the comedian Goldoni, though raised above the level of the square, still seems a companionable part of the life that passes around him, moving in its midst as he moved amid the life of the eighteenth century in Venice, meditating upon it, observing, loving it, faithfully and fearlessly recording it. Marked by a realistic fidelity and insight worthy of a greater age, Dal Zotto's statue of Goldoni is in its own way itself a masterpiece and one of the noblest works of modern art in Venice, full of sympathy and understanding and admirable in execution. The sculptor might seem to have lived as an intimate with Goldoni, and the realism of his treatment suits the subject singularly well. The comedian is not aloft upon a pedestal, remote from men, in glorious aloofness; he is raised but slightly above our heads, not much observed of the crowd, but observing all. Briskly he steps along, in buckled shoes, frilled shirt and neckerchief, his coat flying open, and a book or manuscript bulging from the pocket of it, his waistcoat slackly buttoned, his cocked hat tipped jauntily upon his forehead over his powdered periwig. As he goes he crushes his gloves with one hand at his back and with the other marks progress with his cane. It is a strong, taut little figure, tending to roundness, with a world of suggestiveness in every motion, an admirable mingling of thought and humour in the face that laughs down on this strange, grotesque, conventional, lovable Venice. What a strange contrast is this, of the slippered sage of the eighteenth century, who houses the swallows in the loose folds of his slouch hat, and the armed hero of the fifteenth, whose every muscle is alert, responsive to the stern controlling will! Goldoni is a sage upon a different platform, meditating upon a different world. His Venice is the Venice of Longhi; she has become pedestrian; she has become a theme for comedy. Comedy might have found plentiful food, no doubt, in the Venice that employed Colleoni, the Venice of the first great painters. There is a fund of humour and whimsicality in the strangely fascinating faces of Carpaccio's citizens. Yet try to picture them held up to ridicule by one of themselves upon the stage, and the imagination faints; the thing is inconceivable.

In Goldoni's age the interest of life was shifted to another field, and he stands as the central figure, the leader in a new campaign, representative not of its vices or its vanities or its follies, but of the solid virtues of which these are the shady side. He is one of those happy spirits which the reactionary age of small things produced, not only in Italy but everywhere in the eighteenth century; a spirit of clear, calm insight and capable judgment, neither enamoured of the life of his small circle nor embittered against it, content to live in the midst of it in serenity and truth.

Goldoni, Colleoni, each is representative of a period in the history of the Republic, periods widely separated in temper and in time, and yet related intimately; so intimately indeed that the period of which Goldoni is the master-spirit is actually foreshadowed in the very presence of the superb warrior of the other public square. To study the process of the growth and the decadence of the Republic is to find that there is no convenient preconceived theory with which it will fit in; it rebels against such manipulation, as everything individual rebels against the ready-made. We need rather to look upon Venice as upon a plant that springs and comes to its perfection and fades slowly away, changing and developing in indefinable gradations, showing at every stage some surprising revival from the past, some strange anticipation of the future. In the fifteenth century itself, while the earliest artists were at work for Venice at Murano, and Carpaccio was as yet unborn, Venice already bore about with her the seeds of her decay. In fact, the growth of her art coincides with the slow relaxation of her hold upon the bulwarks of her policy both at home and abroad. The election of Foscari as Doge in 1423 marks a moment of change in Venetian life and government, indicated by the substitution of the title Signoria for that of Commune Venetiarum, and by the abolition of the *arengo*—yet Carpaccio has still his grave citizens to portray, and Ursula sleeping the sleep of infancy. Among the exhortations which tradition has handed down to us as addressed from time to time to the Venetians by Doge or by ambassador is that supposed to have been spoken on his death-bed by Foscari's precursor, the Doge Tommaso Mocenigo. It might have been spoken for our instruction, instead of as a reminder to his own subjects of what they knew so well, so vivid an impression is to be derived from it of the inner life of Venice during the first thirty years of the fifteenth century. Whether legendary or not, these exhortations have something significant and individual about them which really illuminates; it is as if a light were suddenly flashed into a vast room, pressing our vision upon one point, providing a nucleus of knowledge about which scattered ideas and impressions may group themselves intelligibly. Whatever they are, they are not the fabrication of a later time which has lost understanding of the spirit that animated the past. If the portrait they give is imaginary, they have seized upon the salient features and endowed them with a vitality which the photograph, however literal, too often lacks. Mocenigo's farewell address is an impressive portico opening upon a new period in the career of Venice, a strange trumpet-note of ill omen on the threshold of her greatest glory. Behold, he says, the fulness of the life you have achieved, of the riches you have stored; turn now and preserve it; there is peril in the path beyond; there is twilight and decay and death. Your eyes, full of the light, have no knowledge of the shadow; but mine, dim now with age, have known it, and its grip is upon my limbs. Venice heard but might not heed his warnings. The sun himself must rise and fulfil his day and set. Decay is in each breath that the plant draws in; it cannot crystallise the moment; inexorably it is drawn onwards to maturity and death. It was inevitable for Venice that as her strength increased her responsibilities should increase with it; perforce she must turn her face to land as well as sea. She could not remain alone, intent only on nourishing and developing her individual life. In proportion to her greatness she must attract others to her, and the circle of her influence must widen till it passed beyond her own control. The dying words of Mocenigo came too late. A temporary delay there might have been; there was no turning back. Venice had been drawn already into the vortex of European mainland politics, and she could not stand aside. In our own colonial policy we are continually confronted with the problem of aggression and defence. In reality there is no boundary between the two, or the boundary, if it exists, is so fine that the events of a moment may obliterate it. St. Theodore carries his shield in his right hand and his spear in the left; and an old chronicler of Venetian glory interprets the action as symbolising the predominance of defence in his warrior's ideal. Doge Tommaso Mocenigo would have approved the interpretation. But spear and shield cannot exchange their functions. Until the spear is laid aside, it will insist on leading;

and Venice had not laid aside the spear, she had furnished herself anew.

"In my time," says Mocenigo, after a pathetic preliminary avowal of his obligations to Venice and of the humble efforts he had made to discharge them, "in my time, our loan has been reduced by four millions of ducats, but six millions still are lacking for the debt incurred in the war with Padua, Vicenza, Verona.... This city of ours sends out at present ten million ducats every year for its trade in different parts of the world, with ships and galleys and the necessary appointments to the value of not less than two million ducats. In this city are three thousand vessels of from one to two hundred anforas burden, carrying sixteen thousand mariners: there are three hundred vessels which alone carry eight thousand mariners more. Every year sail forty-five galleys, counting small and great craft, and these take eleven thousand mariners, three thousand captains and three thousand calkers. There are three thousand weavers of silk garments and sixteen thousand of fustian.... There are one thousand gentlemen with incomes ranging from seven hundred to four thousand ducats. If you go on in this way, you will increase from good to better, you will be lords of riches and of Christendom. But beware, as of fire, of taking what belongs to others and making unjust war, for these are errors that God cannot tolerate in princes. It is known to all that the war with the Turk has made you brave and valorous by sea, ... and in these years you have so acted that the world has judged you the leaders of Christendom. You have many men experienced in embassies and government, men who are perfect orators. You have many doctors in diverse sciences, lawyers above all, and for this reason many foreigners come to you for judgement in their differences and abide by your decisions. Take heed, therefore, how you govern such a state as this, and be careful to give it your counsel and your warning, lest ever by negligence it suffer loss of power. And it behoves you earnestly to advise whoever succeeds me in this place, because through him the Republic may receive much good and much harm. Many of you incline to Messer Marino Caravello; he is a worthy man and for his worthy qualities deserves that rank. Messer Francesco Bembo is an honest man, and so is Messer Giacomo Trevisan. Messer Antonio Contarini, Messer Faustin Michiel, Messer Alban Badoer, all these are wise and merit it. Many incline to Messer Francesco Foscari, not knowing that he is an ambitious man and a liar, without a basis to his actions. His intellect is flighty; he embraces much and holds little. If he is Doge, you will always be at war. The possessor of ten thousand ducats will be master but of one. You will spend gold and silver. You will be robbed of your reputation and your honour. You will be vassals of infantry and captains and men-at-arms. I could not restrain myself from giving you my opinion. God help you to choose the best, and rule and keep you in peace."

Mocenigo's warning was disregarded. But although Foscari was made Doge, Venice did not rush into war. In spite of repeated efforts on the part of the Florentines to secure an alliance, the traditions of the old peace policy were tenaciously adhered to during the first years of the new reign. It was the temptation to secure Carmagnola as leader of her forces which finally overcame her scruples. Foscari's discourse on this occasion, as reported by Romanin, is a curiously specious mingling of philanthropy and self-interest. Reading between the lines, we understand from it something of Mocenigo's fears at the prospect of his election. The passion of empire is in his heart. Venice, whom eulogists loved to represent as the bulwark of Europe against the infidel, is now to be the champion of down-trodden Florence. It is the sword of justice that she is to wield. We are reminded of Veronese's allegory— Venice seated upon the world, robed in ermine and scarlet, her silver and her gold about her, her breast clasped with a jewelled buckler, round her neck the rich pearls of her own island fabric, on her head the royal crown. Her face is in the shadow of her gilded throne and of the folds of the stiff rose satin curtain, as she looks out over the world, over the universe, from her lofty seat on the dark azure globe. The lion, the sword and the olive branch are at her feet. What is she dreaming of, this Venice of the soft, round, shadowed face? Is it of peace, or of new empire? Is it to the olive bough or to the sword of justice that she inclines? In a neighbouring fresco, Neptune, brooding in profound abstraction beside his trident, deputes to the lion his watch; but Mars of the mainland is alert, on foot, and his charger's head from above him breathes fire upon his brow.

"You will be the vassals of captains and men-at-arms." There was a note of prophecy in Mocenigo's closing words, and it is indeed a question, in face of Verocchio's superb warrior—who was the prince and who the vassal, who the servant and who the master. Colleoni's triumph at his grand reception in Venice can scarcely have been the triumph of a mere man-at-arms. Studying the magnificent reserve of strength in his grandly moulded face and neck, we feel Venice must rather have acknowledged that an Emperor had descended in her midst. Little wonder that such a man dared ask a place on the Piazza of St. Mark itself! The period of his command embraced some of the most brilliant successes of the Venetian arms on land. Difficulties and perils that seemed insurmountable were yet surmounted by a mind possessed of supreme qualities of judgment, daring and nobility. Singularly akin, indeed, to Venice herself was this man who had a key to the minds of his antagonists, who read their secrets and forestalled their actions: it is not strange that he was dear to her. Though a professional soldier and no Venetian born, he could act as a worthy representative of Venice, and there might seem small fear of ruin for a Republic that could so choose her servants. But Colleoni had fought against the Lion and set his foot upon its neck, and the Lion had been constrained to turn and ask his service of him, the highest tribute it could offer, the completest confession of its defeat. And Colleoni could respect and be faithful to such a paymaster: for twenty years he led the Republic on land, and was never called to render an account before her judgment-seat. Magnanimously at his death he absolves her of all her debts to him, makes her two grand donations, then, by his own wish, towers over Venice, a paid alien, her virtual master, yet such a master as she was proud to serve. We wonder if this thought came ever to the mind of Verocchio, the Florentine, as he moulded the great figure of the hero: did the imagination please him of Venice the vassal, Venice subjected beneath the horse and his rider?

There was a fête given in honour of Colleoni at Venice in 1455, on the occasion of the bestowing on him the staff of supreme command. To Spino, Colleoni's enthusiastic biographer and fellow citizen, the episode was portentous, as to one unfamiliar with Venetian traditions in this respect. It had, indeed, a significance he did not dream of; it was the reception not of a victorious fleet, not of an admiring monarch or fugitive pope, but of an army of mercenaries and their leader. Spino tells how Colleoni was accompanied by an escort of the chief citizens of Bergamo, Brescia and other cities of the kingdom that had been committed to his charge; how barges over a thousand were sent from Venice to fetch him and his party from Marghera; how the Venetians came out in flocks to meet him in gondolas and sandolos to the sound of trumpets and other instruments of music, preceded by *three* ships called *bucintori*, "of marvellous workmanship and grandeur," in which were the Doge and Signoria, the senate and other magistrates; and how ambassadors of kings and princes and subject states came to do homage to the new Serenissimo Pasqual Malipiero. He tells, as all the chroniclers of festivals at Venice tell, of the throngs, not only on windows and upon the fondamentas, but upon the house roofs along the Grand Canal; of Colleoni's reception at San Marco and the display of the sacred treasures at the high altar; and how, as he knelt before the Doge, the staff of his office was bestowed upon him with these words, "By the authority and decree of the most excellent city of Venice, of us the Doge and of the Senate, ruler and captain-general of all our men and arms on land shalt thou be. Take from our hands this military staff, with good presage and fortune, as emblem of thy power, to maintain and defend the majesty, the faith and the judgments of this State with dignity and with decorum by thy care and charge." For ten days the festivals continued with jousts and tournaments and feats of arms. But all was not fêting and merriment. Colleoni held grave discourses also with the Padri, and "their spirits were confirmed by him," says Spino, "in safety and great confidence."

IN THE PIAZZA.

The Venice who could thus do honour to Colleoni her general was a superb Venice, superb as Colleoni himself who in his castle of Malpaga received not only embassies from kings but kings themselves; who, at the visit of Cristierino, King of Dacia, came out to meet him "on a great courser, caparisoned and equipped for war, and he, all but his head, imperially clad in complete armour, attended only by two standard-bearers carrying his helm and lance, while a little further behind followed his whole company of six hundred horse in battle array, with his condottieri and his squadrons, all gloriously and most nobly armed and mounted, with flags flying and the sound of trumpets"; who, besides making rich provision for all his children, built churches, endowed monasteries and left to the Venetians, after cancelling all their debts to him, one hundred thousand ducats of gold. The Venice that employed Colleoni was superb—we have a record of her living features in Gentile Bellini's marvellous presentment of the procession in St. Mark's square—the brain as flexible, the jaws as rigid as those of the mighty warrior Verocchio conceived. Yet Spino's comment on the last tribute paid by the Venetians to their general gives us pause—"confessing to have lost the defender of their liberty." It was a confession which could still clothe itself triumphantly in the great bronze statue, but there is an omen in the words. In this confession of 1496 is foreshadowed the fall of 1796.

Much has been written of the social life of this Venice of the Fall; there are countless sources for its history in the letters, diaries and memoirs of its citizens and of its visitors, reputable and disreputable; richest sources of all, there are the pictures of Longhi, the comedies of Goldoni. But of the Venice that lay behind this small round of conventions and refinements, laxity and tyranny, perhaps less has been said. Of many avenues by which it might be approached we shall choose one, and since the praise of Colleoni has drawn our attention to the foundations of Venetian power on land, nothing will better serve our purpose than the foundation of her power by sea, that Arsenal which Sansovino described as "the basis and groundwork of the greatness of this Republic, as well as the honour of all Italy." The Arsenal was, next to San Marco, perhaps the sanctuary of Venetian faith. It was far more than a mere manufactory of arms and battleships. In the celebration of the Sensa its workmen held the post of honour, the rowing of the Bucintoro. Its officers were among the most reputed in the State. The Council of Ten had a room within its precincts. It was entered by a superb triumphal arch, a sight which none who visited Venice must miss. The condition of the Arsenal may well be taken as an index to the condition of Venice herself.

We may set side by side two pictures of the Arsenal, one drawn from a curious little work of early seventeenth century, a time at which, though Venice was moving down the path of her decay, the glorious traditions of the past still found renewal in her present life, and the Venetian fleet was still a triumphant symbol of Venetian greatness; the other from the reports of her officials in the last years before her death. Luca Assarino was one of many guests who had to say to Venice, or to the Doge her representative, "My intellect staggers under the weight of a memory laden with surpassing favours. You received me into your house, did me honour, assisted me, protected me. You clothed yourself in my desires, and promoted them on every occasion; and this not only without having had of me any cause to honour me so highly, but even without having ever seen me." He feels he cannot better discharge the burden of his gratitude than by shaping some of the emotions inspired in him by his visit to the Arsenal. There is a touch of sympathy and sometimes even a touch of truth and insight under the extravagantly symbolic garb of his appreciation. "Admiring first of all an immense number of porticoes, where as in vast maternal wombs I saw in embryo the galleys whose bodies were being framed, I realised that I was in the country of vessels, the fatherland of galleons, and that those masses were so formidable as to show themselves warriors even in their birth, fortifying themselves with countless nails and arming thus their very vitals with iron. I considered them as wandering islands, which, united, compose the continent of Venetian glory, the mainland of the rule of Christendom. I admired with joy the height of their masts and the size of their sailyards, and I called them forests under whose shade the Empire of the sea reposed and the hopes of the Catholic religion were fortified. And who, I said to myself, can deny that this Republic has subjugated the element of water, when none of her citizens can walk abroad, but that the water, as if vanquished, kisses his feet at every step?" Like all recorders of the glories of Venice, he is struck dumb at certain points by fear of the charge of fabling, but, collecting himself, he proceeds to speak of the trophies and relics, the rows of cuirasses, helmets and swords that remained as "iron memorials to arm the years against oblivion of Venetian greatness. What revolutions of the world, what accidents, what mutations of state, what lakes of tears and blood did not the dim lightnings of those fierce habiliments present to the eye of the observer?... I saw the remains of the Venetian fleet, vessels, that, as old men, weighted no less with years than glory, reposed under the magnificence of the arches which might well be called triumphal arches. I saw part of those galleons to which Christianity confesses the debt of her preservation.... And last, I saw below the water so great a quantity of the planks from which vessels afterwards are made, that one might truly call it a treasury hidden in the entrails of a lake. I perceived that these, as novices in swimming, remained first a century below the surface, to float after for an eternity of centuries; and I remarked that they began by acquiring citizenship in that lake, to end by showing themselves patricians throughout the seas, and that there was good reason they should plant their roots well under water, for they were the trees on which the liberty of Venice was to flower." In his peroration the eulogist strikes a deeper note. "May it please Almighty God to preserve you to a longest eternity; and as of old the nations surrounding you had so high an opinion of your integrity and justice that they came to you for judgment of their weightiest and most important cases, so may heaven grant that the whole of Christendom may resort always to your threshold to learn the laws of good government."

We think sadly of his prayer among the records of abuse and corruption in the Arsenal of two centuries later; the Venetian lawyers were still renowned among the lawyers of the world, but the State was no longer capable of teaching the laws of good government to Christendom. The theatre, the coffee-house, the *ridotto*, the gay *villeggiatura* were now the main channels of her activity; the tide of life had flowed back from the Arsenal and left it a sluggish marsh. In the arts of shipbuilding no advance had been made, and the cause lay chiefly in an extraordinary slackness of discipline by which workmen were first allowed to serve in alternation and in the end were asked for only one day's service in the month. Many youths who had not even seen the Arsenal were in receipt of a stipend as apprentices, in virtue of hereditary right. Martinelli tells of porters, valets, novices and even of a pantaloon in a troop of comic actors who were thus pleasantly provided for. There was a scarcity of tools, and even the men in daily attendance at the Arsenal spent their time in idle lounging and often in still more mischievous occupations for lack of anything better to do; disobedience and disloyalty were rife. The Arsenal was used by many as a place of winter resort, as workhouses by the tramps of to-day, and the wood stored for shipbuilding was consumed in fires for warming these unbidden guests, or made up into articles of furniture for sale in the open market. The report of the Inquisitors of the Arsenal, dated March 1, 1874, which Martinelli quotes, is indeed a terrible confession: "One sad experience clearly shows that the smallest concession ... becomes rapidly transformed into unbridled licence. Not to mention the immense piles of shavings, from sixty to seventy thousand vast bundles of wood disappear annually. The wastage of so great a mass of wood, more than the equivalent of the complete outfit of ten or twelve entire ships of the line, is not to be accounted for under legitimate refuse of normal work, but points plainly to the voluntary destruction of undamaged and precious material." It is scarcely surprising that with so little care for the preservation of discipline in the Arsenal and for the efficiency of its workmen Venice fell behind. The Arsenal had indeed become, as Martinelli says, "a monument of the generous conceptions of the past—a monument, like the church and campanile of San Marco, beautiful, admirable, glorious, but as completely incapable as they of offering any service to the State." Similar abuses existed also in the manning of the ships. The officers were for the most part idle and incompetent, and the despatches of the Provveditori are a tissue of lamentable statements as to the depression of that which had been, and while Venice was to retain her supremacy, must ever be, the mainstay of her power. There is desertion among the crews and operatives; the outfit provided for them is unsuitable and inadequate. Nicolò Erizzo, Provveditor Extraordinary to the Islands of the Levant, concludes a despatch, dated October 30, 1764, as follows: "Thus it comes about that your Excellencies have no efficient and capable officers of marine, and if an occasion were ever to arise when it were necessary to send them to some distant part, let me not be deemed presumptuous if I venture frankly to assure you that they would be in great straits. I had a proof of the truth of this when I launched the galley recently built; for the officers themselves begged me to put a ship's captain on board, since at a little distance from land they did not trust themselves, nor did they blush to confess it in making this request."

It was ten years earlier, in 1744, that the Ridotto, or great public gaming-house, was closed in Venice by order of the Great Council, and the Venetians, their chief occupation gone, were reduced to melancholy peregrination of the Piazza. "They have all become hypochondriacs," writes Madame Sara Gondar. "The Jews are as yellow as melons; the mask-sellers are dying of starvation; and wrinkles are growing on the hands of many a poor old nobleman who has been in the habit of dealing cards ten hours a day. Vice is absolutely necessary to the activity of a state." This then is the Venice against which Goldoni stands out; and after all, the essential difference between the world reflected in his comedies and that world of Gentile Bellini and Carpaccio, which was Colleoni's world, is a difference of horizon. There is an epic grandeur about Carpaccio's world:

heroes stride across it, with lesser men and lesser interests in their train. The small affairs of life are not neglected. There is the Company of the Stocking, who discuss their peculiar device and the articles of their order with the grave elaboration of State councillors. Venice was always interested in matters of detail. But in Colleoni's day the same seriousness of purpose was available when larger issues were discerned: in Goldoni's the power to discern larger issues has disappeared. The Venetians, lords once of the sea, can still take interest in their stockings, but they can take interest in nothing else. The Lilliputians are in possession. Goldoni does not quarrel with his age for not being monumental, and we shall do well to follow his example and make our peace with it. He looks upon the clubs of freemasons, the pedantic literary reformers, the false romanticists, the bourgeois tyrants and masquerading ladies, with a serene and indulgent smile. In his famous literary dispute with Gozzi he maintains before his fiery opponent the calm and level countenance of truth. The battles rage around him, but he stands firm and unassailable, as Colleoni himself may once have stood in the midst of battles how different, waged in how different a world!

Chapter Eight
VENETIAN WATERWAYS
(PART I)

IN Venice it is difficult to make choice of one route rather than another, when the means of transit is indeed an end in itself, and in some degree the same delight awaits us on every way we choose. We may pass hours on the Grand Canal merely combining enjoyment of its changefulness with a welcome monotony of rest; every moment the water is expressive, every moment it lives under some new impulse and reveals itself afresh. Carpaccio's picture, *The Miracle of the Holy Cross*, is a marvellous rendering of the life of the Grand Canal; we are reminded of it again and again as we turn into the noble sweep of the waters at the angle of the Cà Foscari. The spirit and motion of Venice seem to be concentrated in the picture—the dark water alive with many gondolas, the fascination of the rhythmic movements of the rowers, at rest or sharply turning or slowly propelling. It has caught and embodied the genius of the canal—that ceaseless change and variation of angle which keeps it springing and full of life; that flowing spirit which unifies the palaces and waters of Venice in a conspiracy of beauty. Our gondola in some mysterious way enrols us in this conspiracy; through its motion we consent to the spirit of the place. We are not onlookers merely; the gondola pulses with the life of Venice; it is an instrument of her being. We feel as we move along that we are needed in the spectacle of Venice, that we have a share in the equilibrium which is of the essence of her power. There is no means of city transit that we can imagine to rival the gondola in its freedom from noise and jostling, in its realisation of comfort. But there are other reasons why it must remain the essential means of passage in Venice. From the gondola alone can we hope to realise how the city stands amid its waters, how living the relation between land and water is. These are not canals in the common sense of the word; they are living streams flowing among islands, each of which is individual, irregular, unique. Venice is not a tract of land cut into sections, large or small, by water, as is an inland city by its streets. A most vigilant watch was kept over the building of the houses that they should not transgress the law of the waters nor interfere with the relation of their currents to the islands. And this vigilance, perhaps, combined with the desire of each owner of land to make use of it to the last fragment, is responsible for the irregularities and varieties of angle which make the houses of Venice more individual than those of any other city. Usually a wall when it has once displayed to us its surface has finished its confidences; it has no reserves, no allurements; it is rigid and uncompromising. But one that breaks from the level, inclining its proud profile in response to the tide of the waterway below it, is a wall of far greater and more individual resources. It is only by gondola that we can appreciate this strong element of personality in the houses, and only by journeying in a gondola that we can learn to appreciate the individuality of the different quarters of Venice. It is not merely that one is peopled by the rich, another by the poor; that one region abounds in ancient palaces, another in modern buildings; nor that peculiar treasures of art are associated with each. Their characters are divergent. From the canals we realise that Venice is built upon separate islands and we see their diversity. The parochial divisions of the sestieri do not exactly follow the shape of the islands, but roughly speaking we shall find the waterways in the district covered by each sestiere distinctive in character. Castello and Cannaregio, San Polo and Dorsoduro, each has its own recognisable method of curve, broad or narrow, wayward or orderly.

VIEW ON GRAND CANAL FROM SAN ANGELO.

The last joy of one who has lived long in Venice, as well as the first of the new-comer, will be a gondola journey. It is impossible to exhaust the certain beauties of even a side canal, not to speak of its casual surprises. If we are in haste and time is precious, we do better to make our way over bridge and calle with what dexterity and speed we can; for it is an insult to ask haste of the gondola. Yet, if we accept in the right spirit the extraordinary delays and dilemmas of traffic—immense, interminable barges suddenly blocking the entire canal, or a flock of gondolas and sandolos in seemingly inextricable confusion—we shall always have our reward; not only the pleasure of watching the riddle of passage solve itself, thanks to the seeming elasticity of the rio, but a glint of sun-jewels on a new angle of the waters, some richness of ornament on house or bridge, some relic of ancient Venice, some name of calle or rio will break upon us with a fresh revelation. We cannot come to the end of Venice; she is inexhaustible: stealing about among the sudden shadows and broken lights of her waterways, sweeping in full, swift tide round unexpected corners and under diminished bridges, some new idea breaks upon us unawares with irresistible persuasion. We cannot define its meaning; we cannot say why details in Venice have so great a significance. A window opened suddenly in one of the palaces at night—why does it seem so portentous? It is another of the manifold gifts of the waters to Venice, this gift of distinction. Venice is not like other cities in which a thousand acts pass unnoted. She has the distinction of a unique individual whose smallest action is fraught with a strange immaterial fragrance that is unmistakably its own. We cannot analyse the fragrance; we only recognise that it is a spiritual gift; it emanates only from subtle and penetrating natures; it is the aroma of life itself. To it we owe the strange excitement that invades us in Venetian waters, and makes a gondola tour far more than a novel mode of traversing a city. As we watch the citizens of Venice from the water, see them crossing a bridge, pausing to lean over, or carried in the stream of passengers, they too seem endowed with a singular vitality; their passing and their standing still appear alike purposeful and portentous. What history might not be written by questioning the windows that look out on the side canals, or the tides that have ebbed and flowed in their channels? It would be a work of many volumes; for the private records of Venice are not lacking in fulness. The Piazza of Bellini's *Procession of the Cross* represents one side of Venetian life, its solemnity, its assurance, its pomp and colour; but the narrow waters know another side, the domestic festivities, the courtings, weddings and banquetings, and private hates. For she was strong in deeds of darkness as in deeds of light, and echoes of them still wash against the basements of her houses. Water is a safer confidant of blood than earth, and the waters of Venice have received their full share of such confidences. Ebbing tides washed out to sea the stains of violence and flowed in to pave the city anew, yet the atmosphere of the dark waterways is more enduring than material stains, and there is no dark deed of ancient Venice to which they may not still supply a realistic setting.

THE LIBRARY, PIAZZETTA.

The gondolier's stock of knowledge will carry us but a small way on the lesser rios. His catalogue is ready for the Grand Canal; he can carry the reader to the obvious points of interest the guide-book enumerates, but his information does not usually comprise even the most beautiful of the palaces of the side canals, and on the more familiar routes there is much to discover for oneself. Moreover there are aspects of a gondola tour which the guide-book cannot include, but which are none the less important for those who really wish to know the physiognomy of Venice. And one is the time of day at which it is to be taken. Venice is the city of light—more luminous than any other city; and if it is true that new light or shadow everywhere alters the aspect of familiar objects, it is infinitely truer in Venice where each moment witnesses the birth of some new and wonderful offspring of the light. If one, who has known the statue of Colleoni against the intense blue of the midday sky, comes on him suddenly when the Campo is in shadow and the Scuola di San Marco alone still receives the light upon the rare marble of its upper façade, he will find that, as the definition of the stern features is lost, a note of tenderness steals into the proud assertion of the face. It seems a fresh revelation of character, this change wrought by a new light in the known and familiar, and it is one of the peculiar creative gifts of Venice.

In considering some of the most noteworthy subjects in the city as she now is, we may imagine a gondola tour on a day of the high tides in December, when the water washes in long smooth waves almost up to the feet of the Lion and St. Theodore, and gives to the Molo the exhilarating effect of a sea-shore. The spring tide spurts and bubbles through the gratings in the Piazza and Piazzetta, to unite in a lake which covers the whole pavement till it deepens in the atrium of San Marco and the heavy outer doors are closed. As the waters rise, the dominion of light is extended; the chequered marbles of the Ducal Palace take on a new brilliance, and the agate eyes of the Lion glow and sparkle as he looks across the sun-paths to the sea. We will imagine ourselves embarking at the Piazzetta and turning into Venice from the Basin of San Marco, under the Ponte della Paglia and the Bridge of Sighs. The entrance into the Rio del Palazzo is flanked on one side by what was formerly the eastern tower of the Ducal Palace. Relics of a Byzantine frieze are all that now remain of it; the rest is lost in the grand eastern wall of the palace—a superb monument of the first Renaissance. This wall would provide material for many hours of study in the rich variety of its sculptures. Not a capital or column is left unadorned, and each is particularised with an apparently inexhaustible variety of design. The two massive, projecting balconies of the Anti Sala dei Pregadi, overhanging the rio, which presented to the sculptor some at least of the problems of ceiling decoration, are richly carved beneath with deep circular roses. The remotest corners are worked with the same conscientious detail as the more conspicuous, and each with a view to its position above the rio. As our eyes grow accustomed to the comparative darkness of the canal, we see that lions look down on us from the arches of the topmost windows, and that some of the upper columns are surrounded by a band of sculpture similar to that on the pillars of the façade of the Scuola di San Rocco. Amid the wealth of sculptured stone there is an impressive severity in the discs of porphyry set at intervals along the wall; but perhaps its greatest beauty is the ducal shield bearing the Barbarigo arms. This shield, placed over a low water-door, is upheld by two winged pages with lighted torches in their hands, who are themselves like songs of light in their graceful and spirited beauty. Massiveness and grace are magnificently combined in this east wall of the Ducal Palace; it is at once solemn and brilliant; and as we look back to its angle with the Riva, the rose and snowy marbles gleam as if they were transparent.

A little further and the waters have us in their power. The Ponte di Canonica denies us passage; the tide is too high for us to pass beneath it, and we are forced to return to the Riva degli Schiavoni. But before we turn we may see one of the most beautiful of Renaissance palaces rising in clear whiteness against the blue of the sky. The Greek marble of its surface is inlaid with circles of serpentine and porphyry; on either side of the central building two scrolls, inlaid with palm leaves, bear the words, *Honor et gloria Deo solo*, and higher in the wall are marble slabs most delicately designed with animals, birds and foliage. A mitre, crown, and crosier, and various other articles of head-dress are represented in the stone, but the Capello family had many branches in Venice, and of the owners of this particular palace even Tassini has no record. The most beautiful of its features is set high up, almost too high to be comfortably seen from the water—two young companion figures of the first Renaissance, full of grace and imagination and strength, each with spear, and scales, and casque surmounted by three heads. These twin warrior angels look out with serene strength into the day; they are lightly armed, but poised and ready for battle. The duplication of their winged figures, and the height at which they are placed, makes us think of them primarily as decorative sculptures; they cannot possess the intimate charm of the young warrior of the Palazzo Civran, but they endow the harmonious marbles of this palace front with a distinction and character which give it rank among the first houses of the greatest period in Venice. After the rains, these precious marbles shine with a peculiar lustre, and the Palazzo Capello as it appears to-day is worthy of comparison with the Palazzo Dario, which glows with serpentine and porphyry beside the Grand Canal, fresh and fine and delicate as on the day of its completion.

CORNER OF THE PALAZZO DARIO.

As the water is still rising and the Ponte di Canonica will not allow room to pass, we must move along the shining waters of San Marco till we find a more hospitable waterway. With difficulty we get under the Ponte del Sepolcro and thence down the Rio della Pietà in which, at the distance of a few strokes, we may land if we will at a low sotto-portico leading to San Giovanni in Bragora, where Cima's noble picture, *The Baptism of Christ*, is imprisoned behind a stifling modern altar which makes it impossible to study the composition as a whole. A little farther, passing a fine ogival palace on our right, we halt before a plastered barocco house with remnants of Byzantine window-posts on an upper story. But our chief interest lies this time in the basement, in a low, narrow arch, the crowns of whose pillars, richly worked in marmo greco with griffins and lions, are, even in time of normal tides, little above the level of the water, though probably the arch once rested on pillars not less than ten feet high. This buried arch is eloquent of the rising of the waters on Venice. It arrests us by the beauty of its workmanship; but it is one of many that we must pass on each canal, though not all have placidly accepted submergence; many have kept above the water by accepting the addition of a capital or crown. Elsewhere there are notable examples of this patchwork of which Venice never is ashamed and which has produced much in her of the greatest interest. In the Salizzada di San Lio, in the sestiere of San Giustina, is a pillar, supporting one side of a sotto-portico, in which a whole page of Venetian history is comprised. Looking into it, we see that it is composed of two distinct portions, that it has in fact two capitals—a capital of the early Renaissance superimposed on a Byzantine column which retains its own. They stand happily united, these children of two ages, but we naturally ask ourselves the reason of their juncture, and the answer is that the Byzantine pillar was once sufficient to itself; it had no need of a crown to complete its dignity or service. No weight of years has shrunk it to these dwarfed proportions. It is the rising of earth from below, not pressure from above, which has reduced it. The soil of Venice has been raised, inch by inch and foot by foot, in defence against her submergence. Many basements have become uninhabitable, and Galliccioli records that in the church of SS. Vito e Modesta an ancient pavement was discovered eight feet below the existing one, while in SS. Simone e Giuda three levels were found one above another. In San Marco a confessional similar to that still at Torcello, after having been lost sight of for several centuries, was found three feet below the soil and one and a half feet below the ordinary level of the water. Our pillar, therefore, which at one time planted its foot firmly on the ground, has been gradually buried alive, and to preserve the serviceableness, as well as the dignity of the portico—in fact, to secure its existence as a sotto-portico at all—a new head had to be added to the Byzantine pillar to supply the theft at its foot. The incident is rich in suggestion of the achievement of the Venetian builders, of the delicate counterpoise and equilibrium, the ceaseless give-and-take required in this city of the sea. Venice was crowned queen, but her dominion could only be maintained by understanding and reverence of the element she ruled. To be glorious she had to be most humble; for the element she constrained is one no human power can subdue; it would kiss her feet, it would endow her with glory, but it would not surrender its life. A thousand times more glorious should be her dominion, but a thousand times more subtle must be her insight and her sway. Her finger must be ever on the pulse of this living force, she must hold the key of its temperament in her hand, she must know when to submit. The wedding of Venice and the sea was not the submersion of one personality in another, it was a union involving infinite tact, infinite insight and acceptance.

We move forward again under the Ponte di Sant' Antonin beside the Fondamenta dei Furlani or Friulani, to the little building at its further end, a sombre little building with heavily barred windows, but with a sculptured façade. Its outer door is never more than half open; it appears to admit visitors reluctantly, and, however bright the sunshine in the world outside, our first impression of San Giorgio dei Schiavoni is always gloomy. Only for two short hours, from ten to twelve in the morning, the chapel is open—short, because the sacristan keeps jealous watch upon the clock and, as if it were with the booming of the great gun from the royal palace that his true day began, hurries to close the remaining wing of the outer door, and bar the chapel into solitude and darkness. Carpaccio's pictures were painted for the light. Their original home was not the Schiavoni chapel, but the School which, till 1451, the Confraternity of St. George and St. Triphonius owned in the convent of San Catterina in the northern extremity of Venice near the Fondamenta Nuova. The chapel of the Schiavoni needs more daylight, and even such as is obtainable is not freely enough admitted; but Carpaccio is a magician whose spell can release us from all consciousness of discomfort. The chapel is an intimate revelation of one of the most fascinating characters in Venetian history. It is the completest record of Carpaccio that exists, the series of paintings in which his imagination has the fullest range. It is not as a portrait painter of Venice and the Venetians that Carpaccio is here employed, his scope is wider and the whole spirit of his treatment is different. The *St. Ursula* series is not lacking in subtle personal touches; but it is not intimate in the same degree as the *St. George*, and it does not touch the level of personal intensity of the *St. Jerome*. There are psychological touches in this chapel of the Schiavoni which it would be hard to rival in modern art; we are companioned here by one of the most humorous, tender, profound and understanding of natures, one who reflects upon life in the spirit of joy and whose painful experiences never prevailed against his assurance of beauty. As is always the case with Carpaccio, each picture, though one of a series, is complete in itself. Except with St. Jerome, the painter shows even a certain carelessness of the preservation of identity in his hero: St. George becomes steadily younger from the time of his combat with the dragon, till, in the third of the series, a mere boy is represented as presiding at the baptism of the king and princess. The figure of St. George in the fight with the dragon is magnificent. No comparisons are necessary to convince us of its greatness of conception; but if we consider for a moment Basaiti's treatment of this subject, we shall understand better the material of which Carpaccio is made. Basaiti's St. George is a sentimentalist even in this moment of stress; his sword-thrust and the spirit expressed in his face are disconnected. With Carpaccio the source of St. George's action is his will. The spirit of the sword-thrust is revealed in the thrilling purpose of his armoured limbs, which no metal can obscure. He is not thinking of graces, but the purpose with which he is instinct creates its own harmony; he is one who must prevail. When the stress of the action is past, his face hardly seems striking, but here it is so pierced with light, as it gleams in paleness against the aureole of hair, that it has become a living flame. Rarely has such glory of purpose and burning intensity of will been conveyed in a human face upon canvas. And all the details of this picture are invested with an accordant beauty. Even the grotesque fancy that seems to riot in the horrors of material death has had to give way before it. The face of the maiden, who lies, half-eaten, close to the dragon's feet, is as exquisite in her death-sleep as that of St. Ursula in her royal chamber; and the mutilated youth under the body of the horse is not less lovely. The horse's face is wonderful; his large eyes drink in the purpose of his master; his tongue lolls; his mane streams wildly as he rushes against the wind. Like Colleoni's horse he triumphs under his rider, not so much ridden as a sharer in his progress; but he, like his master, moves in another and more romantic world than Colleoni. Never was horse more gloriously or more worthily caparisoned; his trappings are of scarlet, stamped with classic heads and chased with bronze; his bridle of the richest gilded leather set with gems. And the dragon too is beautiful. If we compare this trampling, vivid creature of the luminous eyes with the crawling worm against which St. George raises his sword in the succeeding picture, we shall feel something of the meaning of the breath of life. The very colour of his skin seems to have flowed through him with his blood; he is abjectly grey when dragged on to the Piazza. This transformation of the dragon is a great feat, the greater when we remember that even when he first appears, the virtue is beginning to go out of him, his claws are already beating the air with growing impotence. This first picture of the St. George series is the most complete lyric of Carpaccio's that we possess; it is an episode of high romance, and its landscape is conceived in the spirit of romantic fantasy. We have noted elsewhere the treatment of the buildings, the way the city, which at first sight seems of a dreamlike quality, like the port whence St. Ursula's prince sets out, defines itself gradually as a solid, fortified citadel, half hidden behind oriental watch-towers. But we have still to note the inspiration with which Carpaccio has unified these defences with the grand sweep of the coast-line. The huge cliffs which enclose the bay on the left, stretching out to the yellow light, are worthy to rank with those in Turner's *Ulysses and Polyphemus*. The landscape to the right of the bay is freer and more fanciful. A cupolaed duomo crowns the cliff behind the princess. Men and horses move on the huge projecting rock, joined to the main cliff only by a natural arch and by a high-swung delicate bridge. The houses among the trees and the horsemen moving over the dizzy bridge enhance the romantic strangeness of effect. The framing by this rugged arch of a full-rigged vessel upon the open sea is one of Carpaccio's happiest fancies. The devastated shore, the sea flowing into the city, the yellow of the sky above the horizon passing into a troubled paleness of cloud-flecked blue, the wind-driven vessel on the high sea, the suggestion of vast ocean spaces—all these combine in the imaginative grandeur of effect. The second picture of the series, *St. George's Return*, is very different in atmosphere. It is filled with sunlight, the trampling of victory and the sound of music. Its keynote is victorious joy and pomp of festival, sounded in the spacious sunniness of the Piazza and the horizon of slope and mountains beyond; sustained in the buildings that surround the square and the airy pinnacles and balconies crowded with onlookers, and in the flags that fly round the octagonal building winging it with air. The radiant flowered brocades compete with the trappings of the horses to perfect the scene; and through it, and round it, sounds the music of drum and trumpet from the turbaned band which forms a background to the royal party, drawing them, as it were, into the sweep of the central square where St. George officiates. All moves to the measure of glad yet solemn music; here is no lightning stroke, no sudden motion; the muscles of action are relaxed, in slow measure the horses paw the ground. The third picture, *The Baptism of King and Princess*, is still pervaded with music. The musicians lead in the scene; the three foreground trumpeters, conspicuous on the carpeted dais, seem to be trumpeting for their lives. The golden, cavernous trumpet-mouth pointing directly at us has a strangely inspiring effect, seeming to invade us with sound breaking on the heavy roll of the meditative drummer. The music connects itself with the background and helps to widen the horizon. There is not one of these pictures which is not enlarged by the suggestion, at least, of some wide background of nature. Sometimes, as in these jubilant scenes, it enhances and extends the gladness of the festival, sometimes it wings our spirits amid conditions that burden and confine. In the first of the *St. Jerome* series, for instance, where the lion arrives, the first point that strikes us is the obvious humour of the scene, the effect of the entry of this gentlest and most companionable of beasts on the Brethren of the cloister. They do not wait to determine its intentions: it is a lion. It is wounded and asking sympathy, but the Brothers have attention for nothing but their fears. But below the humour there is tragedy. It is not the quaintness of the lion, or the scattering monks, or the beasts on the grassy square, or all the varied monotony of that beautiful frescoed cloister, that claim our attention as the heart of the picture. It is the bent and aged figure of St. Jerome. His features are the same as in the study scene, but his mature youth has given place to snowy age. And another change has come over his face; the radiance of the study scene is replaced by bewildered sorrow slightly touched with contempt. A loneliness is now in his face. In his study he was at peace communing with other minds or with the mind of God. But here with the monks he is bewildered— bewildered and oppressed. We seem to see him ageing as he eyes his foolish companions. Is this, he seems to question, the fruit of his long sojourn? He has asked the sympathy of the Brothers, and they are beside themselves with fear. There is deep pathos in this aged figure making his appeal in vain, and if the cloister filled the horizon, the effect on our spirits would be stifling. But there is a great sky overhead, there is an orange tree, "that busy plant," there is a winding way amidst the vista of palm trees and blue hills, there is the great desert whence the lion has come. *The Death of St. Jerome* affords a still more impressive example of this kind of relief. Here we are not walled in, the desert is around us; we see it through the gateway by the well and through the porticoes of the buildings, and above it in purple outline rise the snow-capped mountains. And this wide horizon is peculiarly welcome as an escape from the confinement of spirit expressed in the funeral procession. The gladness of the open country, the hills and mountains, the palm-tree signposts along the desert way, are a relief to the lion's agony. For the lion is the keynote of the picture, though it is struck so quietly that at first we may even be unconscious of its sounding. In the foreground on a narrow strip of pavement lies the body of St. Jerome. His head rests upon a stone and his long beard lies straight and smooth upon his breast. It is quite lifeless, this body, but the kneeling Brothers think their master is before them. There are wonderful character studies among these Brothers, sensual and simple and devout. Those Carpaccio has chosen to read the Office for the Dead are the most lifeless. The skull on the blasted tree trunk, which his love of the grotesque has inserted in the angle of the wall, seems a fit symbol of the sovereignty they acknowledge. But we have already noted the existence of another actor in the scene. In front of a little group of buildings under a broad rustic portico lies the lion, not inert like his master or like the monks who perform the rites of the dead, not now a suppliant, deprecating lion. His paw tears the ground, his head is raised; he roars in the agony of his bereavement. He is no longer feared, it seems; custom has staled the terrors of him. To the Brothers he is merely another animal of the menagerie, one of the last whims of Brother Jerome. Yet he understands that his master is not here in this square of the convent. He has long been content; but now the desert calls to him and he answers with the voice of the desert that he had unlearned for a while. We have mentioned only a few of the series of paintings in this wonderful chapel, and even of them the greater part has been left unsaid. Each picture requires the whole of the two hours, the Scuola allows, for study of them all; but, in coming to them from time to time for a few moments only, we may constantly discover some new token of their artist's insight and understanding, some richness of composition, some delicacy of colour, some intimate detail of workmanship which makes us feel Carpaccio's presence. The beauties of St. Jerome's study are almost inexhaustible; the details of this exquisite room will reveal to us much of Carpaccio and of Venice. Nothing is in it by chance or because space has to be filled. The gold and rose of the apse, the marble of its pillars, the painted ceiling and richly bound manuscripts, the delicate bronzes, the colouring of the walls, the tiny white dog (forerunner of the lion), the crosier and crimson cushion, all are expressive. And there is one touch—for which we give thanks to the artist—unobtrusive but surely significant; the candles on either wall are held in the bronze fore-paws of a lion. This Chapel of the Schiavoni has not gone unscathed; during a fire that two years ago destroyed a warehouse on the opposite bank of the canal, the water from the engines poured through the roof of the chapel, injuring the pictures on the wall nearest the rio—the *Combat of St. George* and his *Return with the Dragon*.

Leaving the sestiere of Santa Giustina, with its relics of ancient Venice and its famous Palace of the Contarini, on our right, and also on our right, the Church of San Francesco della Vigna, where in the darkness of the Giustiniani Chapel are preserved some of the most beautiful sculptures of the Lombardi, we turn sharply to the left into the Rio del Pestrin, and again to the left into the Rio San Lorenzo. This Rio San Lorenzo is the scene of one of Gentile Bellini's most famous pictures. We are parallel here with the Rio di Sant' Antonin, by which we came from the basin of St. Mark. The miracle represented by Bellini as taking place here is one of those connected with a fragment of the true Cross belonging to the School of San Giovanni Evangelista. Some of the finest artistic power of Venice was lavished in honouring the virtues of this relic, and we owe to it inestimably precious records of the city in the days of her splendour. We understand in watching Bellini's procession something of the nature of those ever-recurring ceremonies which made Casola feel that the Venetians must needs be specially beloved of God. The three-arched bridge of San Lorenzo, which is the structural centre of the composition, is thronged with a white-robed confraternity bearing splendid candles which glint among the trees that are tied upon the bridge, and that we see receding into the campo of the church which is hidden from us. In the centre of the bridge is fixed the banner of the Confraternity, waving in the wind. The throng upon the bridge is by no means idle; there is the effect of that incessant movement of which one is conscious in the densest crowd, and those at its edge are eagerly watching the doings in the water. It is indeed the water that excites our chief interest; Bellini has contrived to perpetuate numberless familiar graces and dignities in the rowers whom we see framed by the central arch of the bridge, or holding up their boats alongside of it. But it is the novel element of the swimmers in the canal which gives the picture a unique place in our regard. In the space of water between the bridge and the temporary platform in the immediate foreground, where kneels a monumental little company of Venetian gentlemen—tradition says the family of the Bellini—is an aquatic display of the most delicate order. Four of the Brothers swim in the clear green water, upheld by their flowing robes like a water-lily by its leaves, and one, the Grand Guardian—as he treads water with admirable equilibrium and an easy grace that is beyond all praise—holds up on high the precious Cross. No words can describe the delight that these swimmers afford us. Their whole heart is in the quest; two of them, an old man and a young, who have been pursuing the elusive trophy in vain, have seen the discovery and slackened their strokes; but one, who has evidently just dived off the fondamenta, is striking boldly out and trying with down-turned face to penetrate the depths of the green water. The negro, stripped, and ready for a plunge, who stands quaking on the lowest step of a wooden landing-stage opposite, affords a delightful foil to the Brothers who swim with such careless proficiency despite their encumbering robes. If he would but look up, he would see that his courage need not be put to the test—that the lost treasure is already sailing triumphantly ashore.

A VENETIAN BRIDGE.

To identify the exact scene of the picture, we shall do well to pass into the Rio San Lorenzo from the Rio del Pestrin and take up our stand a little beyond the Ponte San Lorenzo at about the point of Bellini's wooden bridge. Looking back we have now in front of us the present Ponte San Lorenzo in place of Bellini's beautiful three-arched bridge, spanning the canal between the long fondamenta on our left, and the campo and Church of San Lorenzo, which are still—as in the picture— wedged between the buildings on our right. The minute private fondamenta also, where in the picture kneel two of the foremost of the procession, is still in existence. On our left is the fondamenta in front of Bellini's beautiful frescoed house, and beyond it several houses of irregular heights, as in the picture, while the horizon on this side is still filled by the main features of Bellini's background—another Palazzo Capello bounded on three sides by water, the Rio Pestrin, the Rio San Lorenzo, and the Rio San Giovanni Laterano. The palace retains some of its grandeur; it is easily recognisable by its shape, though to-day it is one storey higher. The Capello arms are still to be seen on it, but it has been robbed of most of its glories of marble and colour. There is a certain melancholy as well as a fascination in attempting to reconstruct the scene of the picture. In the Gallery, when we are face to face with the frescoed houses that we may only see foreshortened, we long to join the spectators across the rio and complete those tantalising fragments of centaurs and figures on horseback that combine with more conventional ornaments to decorate the palace on the fondamenta. But now we are face to face with reality, the frescoes are no more. With the exception of the Palazzo Capello it is only the shape and relative position of the houses that assures to us their identity.

In Bellini's time this corner by San Lorenzo was splendid indeed. The Capello family, which, according to the chroniclers, was numbered among the patricians in 1297, played a prominent part in all Venetian activities, but chiefly in war. It is a member of this family—Vittore Capello, generalissimo of Venice in the Turkish campaign of 1462 and 1465, who is represented as kneeling before Sant' Elena in the beautiful relief above the façade of Sant' Aponal. Another Capello—Vincenzo—in the succeeding century filled five times the office of Admiral, and in 1541 erected the façade of Santa Maria Formosa. Notoriety of a different kind was brought to the family by Bianca, who married for love and freedom, and was cheated of both, but who died Grand Duchess of Tuscany. This palace of the Capello family at San Giovanni Laterano was worthy of their fame. The superb side wall that faces us in Bellini's picture is like a tapestry in diamonds of dusky crimson and gold. It is bordered by a design of gold below the bands of colour, which are most effectively placed immediately under the projecting roof. A beautiful design in red and green, like rich embroidery, forms a kind of flag, enclosing the Capello symbols on a shield painted in different shades of blue. Everything that conventional ornament could do to beautify the house has been done. Ornamental borders and squares are set among the bricks, and the smooth marble facings of the ogival windows are inlaid with coloured discs and knobs. The lower square house at the end of the fondamenta, divided from the Capello palace by the rio, has the same beauties of ornamental band and stripes of alternating colours beneath the roof. The single window in the wall that faces us is magnificent, grated and enclosed by gilt rope-work; the capitals of its pillars and its ogival arch are richly gilded, and in the surface of the stone above are set discs of porphyry with centre and rim of gold. Over the massive wooden entrance door is a painted frieze of green leaves, and discs with Byzantine birds are inserted in the wall above. A grand surface of wall is still left for the fresco painter, and Tintoretto was yet to come. Perhaps the most notable feature in this lower house is the carving of its chimneys; each has an individual form. The fondamenta in the picture is thronged with citizens, and the conspicuous row of stalwart ladies, who kneel on its extreme edge above the water, tradition calls Catterina Cornaro and her train. Certainly this representation of the Queen of Cyprus and her train is different from that which Bembo has given us in his delightful letters to Lucrezia Borgia from Asolo. Catherine, it is true, was no longer a girl when she went to her captivity at Asolo; but there is a lightness and freedom in Bembo's picture of the party who told tales of love and philosophy and idled among the gardens, which leaves us unprepared for the solidity and uncomeliness of this uniform row of figures. We know little of this Queen of Cyprus, but we expect more grace of her than is possible to these matrons. They have studied so little how to please in the wearing of their sumptuous robes, that despite their jewels they produce an effect of almost conventual dulness. It is difficult to imagine anything more magnificent than the dresses of these ladies; they are literally covered with jewels. Excessively virtuous they may be, but they are also excessively lavish; they might well give ground for the legislation as to women's dress quoted by Sanudo; but they have not taught their jewels to shine. The matron who heads the row is robed in dark velvet: her sleeves and the front of her bodice are of gold, slashed with white and trimmed with pearls. An edging of solid gold, studded with jewels, passes from her shoulders to her waist; rich lace completes the decoration of her bodice. Strings of pearls cross on her breast, and a thickly turned gold cord is round her neck and hangs in front. She wears a gold coronet set with gems, and beneath it a broad ornamental band. A transparent veil falls down her back, and is draped about her forehead and neck, covering her long ear-rings. A jewelled cross hangs on her breast, and a chain round her waist. Rings are the only possible splendour she and her ladies are without. The Venetian ladies and gentlemen standing behind this Queen of Cyprus and her train are hardly less sumptuous than they, but their robes are less rigid and uniform, and very much more gracefully worn. The men are dressed in a splendour of brocade and cloth of gold that gives out a rich and sober glow.

We may well feel the inadequacy of words as We attempt to revive this wonderful painting. Bellini faithfully recorded

Venice, but we cannot so faithfully record Bellini. We can only hope to call attention to the detail of what is undoubtedly one of the most valuable portraits of the Venice of the first Renaissance by one of the greatest of her citizens. When we have paused long enough on the site of the picture and go down the Rio San Giovanni Laterano, immediately in front of the Capello Palace, the high water again denies us passage; but it gives more than it withholds in compelling us to return to our former junction with the Rio Pestrin and to pass out among the coal barges making the wider circuit of the lagoon. It is a wonderful moment when we come suddenly from the narrow water into the wide expanse of the lagoon; and on this December morning a marvellous vision awaits us. The long brown line of Sant' Erasmo lies like a dark cloud on the water; Burano, San Francesco and Torcello are isolated in a strange translucency of mist; whilst from the low tones of the water one red sail rises like a column of flame. Above Murano the smoke coils languidly; the cypresses over the cemetery wall stand out in startling blackness. A flock of gulls incessantly flickers and glitters on the surface of lucent aquamarine that stretches away to the shore where the mountains lie like purple shadows crowned with a radiancy of snow. The sunlight of the lagoon in this wintry clearness seems other than that which falls on the waterways of the city; this outer robe of Venice to-day is of so immaterial a texture that we feel the material city slipping from our grasp. We turn back into it, but by a way that can feed the visionary sense, by the Rio dei Mendicanti. It might seem, indeed, that all vision would die in the dreary, plastered uniformity of the building that stretches along the fondamenta on our left. This building was formerly the Scuola di San Marco; but the superb façade erected by the Confraternity on the Campo di SS. Giovanni e Paolo has little in common with these white-washed walls and dreary sunless corridors. For this most famous School is now the Hospital of the Mendicanti, and it is as a visitor to the wards that we are admitted. Yet amidst these chill cloisters and corridors is kept one of the most luminous and visionary treasures of Venice—Tintoretto's *Procession of St. Ursula and The Virgins.* It is the more precious as being, with *Bacchus and Ariadne* and *The Paradise,* almost the only work of Tintoretto that we can make sure of fully seeing. There is abundant light in the cold, grey church to illumine a picture which is in itself a song of light in the daybreak.

This stream of wonderful maidens moves all to one rhythm, winding with sweeping trains down out of the misty dawn to end and centre in the glorious figure of St. Ursula waiting the bishop's consecration of her mission. She is so entrancingly radiant that the young cross-bearing bishop who stands beside her seems, as he gazes, to be illumined by her fire and joy. The ships in which the company is to embark lie like phantoms on the misty sea-line, and the long lights of dawn are above the water—pale rose and gold and purple—while the curtain of night is slowly withdrawn, leaving spaces of darker blue and glowing cloud. The early morning mists still hang about the shadowy hulks of the huge vessels and the figures near the shore, making as it were two spheres of action. The grassy slope down which the travellers come, seems in its undulations to yield itself to their motion, to reflect and echo it, and is luminous as all the figures are. The faint rainbow raiments of those distant companies that sweep forward nearer to the shore are like wings lit from the dawn and half-folded, while the foremost ranks of the procession are in the full golden light of day. Note with what daring Tintoretto has placed the strong rose-robed angel with the palms of martyrdom across the picture directly overhead. Her figure cuts across the phantom ships; one arm hides part of the procession; yet far from obscuring or diverting from the central theme, she leads the eye more directly to St. Ursula. There are no spectators of this morning procession, unless it be the marvellous group on the left. The central figure is that of a woman, meditative, gathered into herself; she scarcely seems to belong to the procession; she is dreaming apart with downbent face, and is very close in feeling to Carpaccio's sleeping St. Ursula. Beside her is a radiant youth, his face one of Giorgione's faces, in a helm shaped like a shell and set with pearls. There are many types of Venetian ladies in the procession, such as were idealised by one and another of the painters; all are here, in marvellous richness of raiment and jewelled headgear. We do not question whether they are fitly robed for a great journey; we only share in their joy. The wine of dawn seems to have entered into them, and to sing in every motion, every colour of the superb lyric—the intoxication of embarking on a mystic voyage in the pale radiance of dawn.

We pass out again through the long corridors under the great sculptured portal. On our left is the church of SS. Giovanni e Paolo, a storehouse of Renaissance art, and before us the friend of whom we never grow weary—Colleoni astride of his war-horse in the centre of the square. This paid servant, this adopted son of Venice, is not on the Piazza where it was his wish to be; but he stands even more fitly here upon this small campo beside the canal. Anywhere he would be monarch; but we are admitted here into his private presence-chamber, while the great stirring Piazza would seem but the crowded outer court. If, before leaving the campo, we make a short journey on foot along the Salizzada which passes on the south of SS. Giovanni e Paolo, we may find a treasure buried in dirt and neglect. None would guess its presence; but those who care for unfrequented paths may venture under the unattractive sotto-portico which leads to the outer staircase of a once beautiful Renaissance palace. It is given over to the poor, but a sculptured doorway still surmounts the stair; its chief beauty however is a series of delicately sculptured arches in the brickwork below, and a fine well-head half imprisoned by the chimney of a neighbouring bakery. The wall of the bakery is so near the staircase of the palace that we can get no complete conception of the arches, and the dirt and ill odours of this neglected corner are likely to daunt all but the most enthusiastic seekers after treasure. Yet these fragments, in elegance and beauty of design, may rank with the worthiest remains of the Venetian Renaissance.

PALAZZO SANUDO.

Returning to Colleoni's square, we again embark and continue our way down the Rio dei Mendicanti, past courtyards flooded by still rising water, and turn soon to the right, into the Rio Santa Marina—a picturesque canal, ever varying in width and angle. At the corner of the Palazzo Pisano we are confronted again by the problem of the high water. If we would include in our tour the Palazzo Sanudo, with its riches of many ages, Byzantine, early Gothic and Ogival, its two courtyards, its beautiful garden on the fondamenta and its dolphin-shaped knocker, we must turn to the right along the Rio delle Erbe. But it is useless to hope that this morning any gondola will be able to pass under its low bridges, and in consequence we must continue our way to the church of the Miracoli, by skirting the other side of the lozenge-shaped island on which it stands. We soon turn at right angles into the Rio dei Miracoli, and in a few moments we see the sun shining on the cupola of the church, gilding the marbles of the circular east tower and lighting the traceries of serpentine and porphyry and cipollino on the west front. It is a joyous and radiant aspect, this of the Miracoli, with its broad spaces of Greek marbles and its bands of Verona, its plaques of verd-antique and porphyry, its sculptured angels and grave apostles. It stands in quiet beauty on the brink of the canal. From its little campo opens the beautiful inner courtyard of the Sanudo Palace, while on another side it is bordered by the spacious and noble Corte delle Muneghe, formerly known as the Corte Cà Amadi, from the family whose arms are still to be seen on the brickwork. Close to the well in this court stood originally the image of the Madonna, thanks to whose miracles we now possess this most beautiful church built in her honour. The chronicles relate that a certain Francesco Amadi, an inhabitant of Santa Marina, had piously set up an image of the Virgin close by his house. The fame of this image as a worker of wonders grew so great that it was transferred by Angelo Amadi, in 1480, to the Corte di Cà Amadi, and set up there for popular veneration. In his Venetian Annals for 1480, Malipiero thus briefly relates the occurrence: "This year began the cult of the Madonna of Miracles which was at the door of Corte Nuova, opposite the door of the Amai in the narrow calle, and because of the crowd of people it became necessary to move the image, and carry it to the courtyard of Cà Amai, and immense offerings have been made of wax, statues, money and silver, insomuch that it has reached four hundred ducats in one month. And in process of time it amounted to three thousand ducats of alms, and with them we bought Corte Nova from the houses of the Bembo, Querini and Baroci, and there was built a most beautiful temple and convent, into which we put the nuns of Santa Chiara of Murano." The foundation-stone was laid on February 25, 1481, when the image was moved with great pomp from the court to the little wooden shelter on the site chosen for the church. An interesting account of the move is contained in the *Memorie* of Angelo Amadi. It affords a vivid verbal picture of religious festivals in Venice at the time they were finding their most splendid expression on canvas. "On the day of the twenty-fifth of February," begins Amadi, "in the name of Messer Jesus Christ and of the glorious Virgin Mary, we removed the image from our house to transfer it to the hut or house of wood where the chapel or church is to be made; at which removal were present all the Schools or Fraternities, the

Battudi, that is, the School of Madonna Santa Maria della Misericordia, to which I belong, and the School of the Carità, and of San Marco, and that lately founded of San Rocco, whose brothers go about in sackcloth, beating themselves continually with scourges and iron chains." All the Procurators of San Marco, he says, were present, with countless cavaliers and doctors and a great part of the Signoria, the Patriarch in his pontificals, and a host of vicars and canons and other clerics, all richly and splendidly clothed. The Amadi insisted on themselves carrying the portable stand that had been made for the image, covered with cloth of gold, cremosine and cloth of silver, and adorned with silver candelabra and oriental censers. "Nor would we allow any other to carry it, that we might demonstrate publicly that it belonged to us and had been made by our ancestor." Four citizens accompanied the image-bearers, carrying poles on which to support the stage as it mounted bridges or stopped in the streets. It was followed by the dignitaries already enumerated and almost the whole Venetian populace. The procession left the house of the Amadi to the sound of trumpet and pipe; it made a circuit of the bridges, streets and squares of the city as far as Santa Maria Formosa, halting in the parish church of the Amadi for many lauds to be sung. "And along all the calli and in the squares of the churches all the people kneeling on the ground prayed devoutly with tears and hands joined on their breasts, calling aloud and raising a great outcry." In this manner the procession returned to the shelter, and the foundation-stone was laid by the Patriarch amid the chanting of lauds. After a final *Te Deum* the image was left to the devotions of the people who, till night fell, continued to pour out their offerings for the building. There is something stirring in this ceremony with its popular outcry and petitions for mercy. It reminds us of that strong element of piety which in Venice went side by side with its strong commercial instincts.

The church of the Miracoli seems to belong peculiarly to Venice in the light of these stories of its birth. It is itself one of the miracles, this little Roman temple; with its quadrangular-domed choir, raised high above the nave, its marble ambones, its dark painted roof, and walls lined with marbles, it impresses us with a sense of sublimity. All here is perfectly proportioned and decorated with simple and absolute fitness. It is impossible to mount the flight of marble steps leading from nave to choir, past the wonderful little figures of St. Clare and St. Francis with his profound contemplative smile, past the Annunciation Angel and the Virgin draped like a Roman matron, into the choir where the great cross of porphyry and serpentine hangs in the apse, without feeling that we are mounting to sacrifice in a temple full of the Deity. But what part has that marvellous little company of sea youths and maidens in the tale of the Passion? They are the offspring of some delicate fantasy careless of all save itself, yet they seem to need no other passport than beauty to their place in the temple. Work of the same imaginative quality is to be seen on a pillar in the nave: not here a dream of mermaids with delicate breasts and arms and glittering tails, but a purely naturalistic subject. The artist has conspired with the stone to sing his delight in the life of the fields, and he has achieved his purpose so that the very spirit of the wild creatures lives again. A lizard with smooth scales and lithe, restless tail, ears of corn, a serpent holding a bird by its look as it rears itself for a spring, birds fighting and birds preening their breasts,—all these delicate beings, that move amid a design of admirable grace, are a field pilgrim's scrip laid open for all who will read. These old artists were not afraid. To them all things of nature appeared symbols worthy to lay on the altar. And it is because of this permeating imaginative vision that the Church of the Miracoli is one of the jewels of Venice, instinct with life, from the grave mystery of its marble-lined walls, slab alternating with slab, Carrara cream and white, paonazetto, marmo greco, marbles of Verona red and almond, to lizard and serpent, siren and infant, from the dusky gold and colour of the ceiling to the eloquent figures that stand in constant ministration on the ambones.

Santa Maria dei Miracoli might well mark the limit of our tour; but if we go a short distance further into the Rio San Canciano we shall come on three examples of the earlier domestic architecture of Venice, which we shall do well not to miss. The first is a house by the Ponte Widmann, dating from the ninth century. It is exceedingly picturesque, with its long, low portico, and a profusion of Byzantine ornaments of most varied device on the walls—weird lions and birds and oriental beasts. The capitals of the window columns also are Byzantine, though the balconies are Renaissance. We can also distinguish, though it is immured, the ancient solario, or sun-terrace, which, in this house of old Venice, was evidently of considerable beauty and extent. Passing under another bridge after the Ponte Widmann, we come to the Ponte Pasqualigo, and landing at the calle on the left, we have on the right of us, only a few steps down, one of the oldest houses in Venice. So well cared for is it by its present owners that we seem not to be examining a relic, but to move in a living page of the past. On the morning we saw it, the sun was streaming into the court and falling on the Signora, who, in scarlet shawl, and with a brilliant kerchief round her head, was dozing in the sun. She rose and gave us a cordial welcome, and we climbed the outer stair, under an immense projecting roof, into the garden hanging above the court, full of sunshine and flowers; higher still, on the altana, was a bright line of clothing hung out to dry. The structure of the ancient roof overhanging the stair is very remarkable, with its secondary beams that jut horizontally under a long cross-beam running the whole length of the gallery. The rooms, which open out of one another from the terrace, are rich also in beams, though now for the most part covered with a foolish uniformity of ceiling. The floor of the reception room is, as usual, paved with small variegated stones, but it is remarkable for occasional little islands of mosaic, one of which, a tiny square of deep blue and gold set diamond-wise, is a veritable gem of colour. Worthy to rank with this hospitable, ample house of ancient Venice, is a courtyard opening on the water, into which we pass immediately from the Ponte Pasqualigo. The wooden barbicans of the projecting roof adjoining the portico rest on pillars of fine earliest Gothic, grave and strong and simple in their build. The sense that they are individuals bearing the burden of the beams is increased by the fact that it is not geometrically adjusted to their shoulders. It rests there because they are willing; there is an understanding, a *combinazione* between beam and pillar, but the two were not mechanically made to fit.

A SIDE CANAL.

Returning to the Rio dei Miracoli we leave the church on our left, and crossing the Rio Santa Marina and the Rio San Giovanni Grisostomo, we pass directly into the Rio del Teatro, leaving the water-entrance to Marco-Polo's palace on our right. This corner is one of the most beautiful in the canals of Venice. It is rich in palaces and fragments of ancient ornament, and full of strange interplay of lights from the many tortuous ways that converge here. There is a constant fascination in the broad sweep of water at the crossways, in the problems of traffic, in the warning cries that herald boat or barge passing under the many bridges. There is perhaps no spot in Venice so full of ancient mystery, of the gloom, the light, the sound and stillness of her waterways. A little further on we pass into the Rio della Fava, full also of delightful and unexpected corners; and looking back from the Ponte di San' Antonio we see the site of

Mansueti's picture commemorating another miracle of the Holy Cross; or rather we see one corner of the picture; for Mansueti has cut away the whole length of a calle and all the houses between this bridge of San' Antonio and the Campo di San Lio, so that in his painting, for obvious artistic reasons, the waters of the canal flow directly in front of the campo, which he has narrowed to little more than a fondamenta. In a sketch for this picture now in the Uffizi at Florence, Mansueti has more faithfully transcribed the actual surroundings of the Campo di San Lio. His picture illustrates a miracle of the Cross that would seem to offer small scope for artistic treatment. A member of the Confraternity of San Giovanni Evangelista, on being invited by another Brother to attend the Cross in procession, impiously replied, "I will neither accompany it, nor do I care whether it accompanies me." Within a short while, continues Flamino Corner, the perverse man died and the School assembled for his burial; but when the procession reached the Ponte di San Lio, the parish of the dead man, the Holy Cross became so heavy that no force could avail to move it. While all stood appalled and dismayed by such an occurrence, the friend of the dead man recalled the impious words he had spoken, and made known the reason of the refusal of the Cross. It was removed from the procession, and, the chronicler informs us, withheld henceforth from any but public solemnities. In Mansueti's composition a number of Brothers are gathered on the bridge attempting to drag the Cross, and the clergy of San Lio and a group of citizens are waiting on the campo to receive it. There is much quaintness in the rendering of this rather humorous incident, and the picture is full of rich and homely detail, in the houses and in the doings of their inhabitants, the chase of a cat, the hanging of a clothes line, the stacking of the pliant rods on which the clothes are hung. The windows, with closed or open gratings, are thronged with onlookers, chiefly splendid ladies. In Bellini, the windows are unpeopled, but here there is scarcely one uncarpeted, and without its contingent of festive heads and shoulders; whilst in one of the windows, in the house we can still identify, a fascinating infant prances against the grating and pokes a fist through the bars. The bridge in the picture is obviously too low for any gondola to pass under it; it is merely a temporary private way thrown across the rio, which it is easy to believe that Mansueti has substituted in order that we may see above it the procession winding out of the Rio del Piombo.

As we look back from the Ponte San' Antonio we may get, in spite of Mansueti's changes, a distinct impression of his scene; the sun, shining through the small circular ogival window in the house that still bounds our horizon, lights up a gay interior of green walls draped in crimson and gold with singular richness of effect.

THE GONDOLIERS' SHRINE.

The name of the Rio della Fava, the Canal of the Bean, boasts a traditional derivation that throws a curious light on Venetian pieties. It appears that in 1480, the same year in which was initiated the cult of the Madonna dei Miracoli at the Cà Amadi, another wonder-working image, under the patronage of the same family, was thought worthy of a chapel in San Lio. This chapel was named Santa Maria della Consolazione, or della Fava, from its proximity to the Ponte della Fava. "The ecclesiastical writers," says Tassini, "recount that the bridge was so named because a man living by it, who had hidden some contraband salt under some sacks of beans, a vegetable he dealt in, when warned that the police were approaching threw himself at the feet of the said miraculous image for succour and obtained this favour—that the Justices, despite their search, found nothing in the house but simple beans." This naïve faith in the willingness of the Madonna to meet all contingencies survives among the humbler citizens of Venice to-day. A proof is provided by the personal experience of a friend who had bespoken overnight a gondola for the station in the dark early hours of the next morning. The gondolier duly arrived and set out with his fare from San Marco. But they had gone no further than the church of the Salute when his lamp gave out and he halted and asked leave to replenish it. No place for procuring oil was apparent, but the gondolier knew one. He went to the shrine of the Madonna and addressed the figure thus, "Blessed Madonna, thou thinkest harm of no man and thou wouldst not that harm should come to any. I turn to thee for help in my need. The police are not like thee. They will have no pity in their fine if they see me at the station with my lamp unlit. I beg thy lamp for this little while." And, as there was-no sign of refusal, the Madonna's lamp was taken to the station and returned on the homeward journey.

Continuing our way down the Rio della Fava we pass almost immediately, on the left, the Palazzo Gussoni, a palace the great beauty of which cannot be overlooked. It is a building of the first Renaissance combining extreme richness of detail with simplicity of general effect. The basement is beautifully and variously sculptured and surmounted by a band of Verona marble; above it rises a design of leaves and ears of corn growing and spreading like a plant, and full of graceful and delicate fancy. The unique feature of the palace is the richly sculptured stone barbacan that supports the projecting portion of the upper storey overhanging the Calle della Fava. There is in Venice an abundance of fine wooden barbacans, but this is the only example we remember of the sumptuous casing in stone.

A little further and we pass below a palace of the Transition, from whose graceful balcony keep watch a row of sculptured lions in half-relief. As we come into the Rio della Guerra, the midday light plays reflectively on the water, striking out of it a thousand fitful diamonds, and the now ebbing tide washes with a soft caressing sound against the houses. At the juncture of the Rio della Guerra with the Rio del Palazzo is the Casa dell' Angelo so named from the beautiful sculptured angel on the wall that faces us. It stands erect, with wings spread, holding in the left hand a globe signed with the Cross, which it seems in the act of blessing. The lower part of its body is covered with two shields bearing, according to Tassini, the arms of the Narni family. It is sheltered by a pent-roof, supported on graceful pillars, most delicately and nobly worked. In the lunette above the angel, in the immediate shadow of the roof, is discernible a painting of the Madonna and Child between two kneeling angels, which still retain traces of soft and beautiful colouring. But the most precious possessions of this palace front are the remnants of fresco under the broad projecting roof at the further end of the building. The beautiful figure of a woman, with head resting on her hand and braided golden hair, is still intact. There is another fine figure between the windows, and there are many fading fragments in the plaster below. Tradition unanimously attributes these frescoes to Tintoretto, and it is difficult to believe that the lovely woman could have come from any other hand.

The Ponte Canonica, which adjoins our first Capello Palace, now allows us an easy passage, and we can take our way on the ebbing tide down the Rio del Palazzo. Below the sombre weight of the Bridge of Sighs, between the palace and the prison, we pass again into the aureole of Venice. Within the brilliant bay formed by the Riva degli Schiavoni the gulls are making festa, and away towards the city they whirl and drift like shining snowflakes in the radiance of the Grand Canal. As we pass the Piazzetta to land at the Molo, the golden sword of Justice gleams superbly luminous in the blue above San Marco. Venice has put on her glory.

Chapter Nine
VENETIAN WATERWAYS
(PART II)

THE centre of our second tour is an ancient and comparatively unfrequented region in the north of Venice—that part of Cannaregio over which watches the Campanile of the Madonna dell' Orto, with its crowning image of snowy stone and four solemn apostles looking out over city and lagoon. The beautiful figure of the Madonna, round whose feet, between the tiles of her ruddy cupola, spring little plants the birds have sown, rises day after day triumphant out of the duel between sun and mist, a pledge of the victory of light; and through all vicissitudes of weather she is seen, sometimes in dazzling outline upon the deep blue, or against a canopy of grey, sometimes herself tempered to shadowy greyness by the brilliance of the cumuli that out-rival even her snowy purity.

We will enter from the Grand Canal by the Rio San Marcuola, nearly opposite the Correr Museum, and pass below the Ponte dell' Anconetta on the Strada Nuova, or more properly the Corso Vittorio Emanuele, which in its broad and ungracious uniformity is one of the most forbidding streets in Venice. It seems at first to have no reserves into which by a little tact or sympathy we may ingratiate ourselves; yet many activities generally to be encountered in other raiment and under other auspices, lurk behind its mask. On this very Rio San Marcuola is a workshop where antiquities are fabricated for the show-rooms of the Grand Canal. We see them here in their early stages, a rude stone well-head awaiting an ancient sculpture, a Renaissance chimney-piece, a Byzantine lion in Verona marble; and the forger is no villain but an honest, genial workman skilled to do better, but content to supply what he is asked for. A little beyond the bridge we come on one of the oldest squeri or boat-building yards of Venice. Black sprites of boys pass to and fro, plunging their torches into cauldrons of burning pitch, to draw them in the wake of flaming branches along the upturned sides of the gondolas; and men, with something of the fire and of the blackness in their eyes and faces, swink like the skilled demons in Spenser's cave of Mammon. It is outside, on the squero, that this coarser work with pitch and cauldron goes on; in the inner workshop are the frames of gondolas in making, exquisite skeletons with subtle apportioning of oak, elm, nut and larch, and long unbroken sides of beech. Opposite the squero, on our right, is the ugly new brick wall of Paolo Sarpi's convent. Above it may be seen a weed-grown fragment of the ancient building with its relief above the door. Boni has suggested that a more appropriate memorial to Sarpi's memory than the erection of a bronze statue might have been the preservation or renewal in its original beauty of the old convent with which he was so closely and intimately connected.

ENTRANCE OF GRAND CANAL.

We strike almost immediately into the Rio della Misericordia, and as we look down the long vista to right and left of us, under the low bridges, we begin to realise the peculiar character of this district. It is entirely different from that of our first tour; long parallel canals run from east to west, cutting the land into narrow strips and giving the strips a curious effect of isolation. These canals are bounded on the west by the lagoon, and the effect of sunset light flooding the long waterways is strikingly beautiful. If we were to follow the Rio della Misericordia to the left, we should come to the curious wedge-shaped island of the Ghetto Nuovo and the tall deserted houses of the Ghetto Vecchio. But we will tend only slightly to the left, and passing under a low bridge continue our former course into the Rio della Sensa. This name has in it echoes of historic festivals; it originated in the fact that the stalls for the great Ascension fête on the Piazza were stored in the warehouses that stood on its banks. As late as the last celebration of this famous offshoot of the Sposalizio festival, in the year 1776, fifty-seven thousand ducats were spent on erecting the enclosure in which the stalls were set up. The Rio della Sensa has many links with the past. Above a door in a humble wall on the fondamenta hangs a shield on which is sculptured an arm cased in steel. This shield belonged to the Brazzo (Braccio) family, of Tuscan origin, who had settled in Venice and acquired much land in this district. The name is worthy of preservation; for one at least of the family has left an enduring mark in the annals of the city. "In 1437," we read in Tassini's *Curiosità Veneziane*, "a Geoffrey da Brazzo, with some companions, founded, in the Campo di SS. Giovanni e Paolo, the Scuola di San Marco of which he was the Grand Guardian." Within the unpaved court the house of the worthy Geoffrey is still standing, and it preserves its early Gothic and Byzantine features but little obscured by later additions. It is not altogether gloomy though evidently inhabited by very poor people; little gardens still blossom from the leads and window boxes, and tables and chairs are set out under the vine in the yard below. In the seventeenth century the family became extinct, its history being closed by a rather sordid domestic tragedy; and it is pleasanter to revert to the earlier days of this simple, dignified citizen's dwelling when Geoffrey and his associates discussed in it the hopes and fears of their School. Another page of Venetian history lies open for us at the Campo dei Mori further along the same rio to the right. Our attention is attracted at once by a curious figure in oriental turban, with a pack upon its head, at the corner of the square which strikes the fondamenta. Two more figures in the same style of dress are stationed at other corners of the square. The crowd of urchins who throng round us the instant we alight will tell us that these are Sior Rioba and his brothers. The key to these figures is to be found in a palace, the inner court of which opens on our right hand as we turn inwards from the canal. It belonged to three Greek brothers, by name Rioba, Sandi and Afani, of the family Mastelli, who leaving the Morea in the twelfth century, on account of disturbances there, came with great wealth to Venice and built themselves this house by the campo which has preserved their origin in its name. This family also has a noble record in Venetian annals. It took part in the Crusade of 1202, and received citizenship for its reward. Later it rested from its labours and set up a spice shop in Cannaregio at the sign of the Camel. From these avocations it passed to a more reposeful existence on the banks of the Brenta, and, like the da Brazzo family, it became extinct in the seventeenth century. The courtyard of the palace, known now as the Palazzo Camello, possesses many fascinating reminders of its past, though some of its old beauties have been taken from it even in recent years. The open arches of the sotto-portico have been filled in, and a corkscrew stair is now only recognisable by the pillars we see immured in a circular tower. The pillars that once supported the arches of the entrance portico, now half buried in the ground from the constant raising of its level, are fine and uncommon examples of the transition from Gothic to Renaissance. Above the portico are two striking projections of carved stone, once serving perhaps to support a lantern or coat of arms, and in the angle of this wall and the main building are the relics of a Gothic pedestal on which, without doubt, some image has stood. The low-beamed court to the water is still intact with its finely-carved architraves and early Gothic pillars; but beyond the point of its present habitation it has been allowed to fall into decay from the invading damp. If we venture along this outer court to the water's edge, we shall find ourselves in the Rio della Madonna dell' Orto almost opposite the campo and church. By the help of a barge which we may reasonably hope to find moored alongside the water-door of the court, we obtained a view of the most characteristic aspect of the Palazzo Camello. The passer-by on the fondamenta cannot fail to be impressed by its beautiful decorative balcony and windows and the Byzantine frieze in a lower storey, but above all by a camel and driver sculptured in admirable relief on the wall.

Returning to the Campo dei Mori, we make our way again to the Fondamenta della Misericordia, where we disembarked. Almost immediately on our left, backing the Palazzo Camello, and perhaps originally forming a part of it, is the house of Tintoretto. It is still unspoiled of its ancient decorations of small sculptured figures and formal designs; and, above all, it is interesting architecturally for its elaborate carved wooden cornice on the two upper storeys to which time has given the appearance of stone. Howells, in his description of Tintoretto's house, conveys an impression of sordid desolation in the building and its inmates. It may lately have fallen on better days; for there is now nothing forbidding about it, and indeed it is a welcome refuge from the swarms of dirty and discordant children whom the presence of a stranger on this campo seems to have a peculiar power of attracting. Its upper windows look out across the rio on a garden with a majestic cypress tree, and down the long canal to the wide waters of the lagoon. And some of the inmates of the house still have a share in the ancient, though humbler, arts of Venice. There are beadmakers working, as usual in almost total darkness, in an airless room in the basement. After we have seen these rows of patient, crouching workers, bending hour after hour over their gas jets, the beads of the lamp-lit Merceria will call up irresistibly the low benches, the glittering wires, the glazed and darkened windows. For there seems a strange irony in the birth of these shining toys out of the gloom. Many unacknowledged artists have worked upon these beads; much, no doubt, of their workmanship is mechanical; but if we look into them we shall find many little originalities in the gradation of line and colour, many touches of taste and feeling in their graceful and various designs. The house is much as it might have been in Tintoretto's day, but the walls seem empty and unresponsive and to have less part in him than those palace fronts in which some faded fresco bears witness to the magic of his hand. But there is a building near by that may rightly be called the house of Tintoretto, where we may more faithfully commune with his mind—the Church of the Madonna dell' Orto, in which, Ridolfi tells us, Tintoretto worked for his keep alone "because his fertile brain was constantly boiling with new thoughts," and thereby roused the wrath of his fellow artists. It was here that Meissonier, coming in his old age to Venice, set himself down at the feet of the master and copied Tintoretto's *Last Judgment* in the choir. But it is not primarily for the artist's great works in the choir that we return again and again to the Madonna dell' Orto. It is for a painting no less the work of a giant, but of a giant gifted with tenderness equal to his strength. The *Presentation of the Virgin* has been moved from its original place on the organ to a side chapel in which both light and space are inadequate, so that, coming on it first out of the daylight, we receive only a vague impression of its greatness. It is only gradually that it breaks on us in its combination of vigorous motion and life with sublime repose, and that we come to distinguish the elements that make up its power and to appreciate the singleness and intensity of vision which, amid all its wealth of resource, never wavers in loyalty to the central idea. In Titian's *Presentation*, the mountain background, the crowd of Venetian citizens, the old egg woman, the Virgin, the

High Priest, appear as separate interests; in Tintoretto's *Presentation* all the elements are unified; there is but one moment, one point, to which everything tends. The lovely women in the foreground, the mighty figures reclining on the stair, the mysterious trio behind in the shadow of the balustrade, all subserve the quiet, yet passionate drama enacted above in the meeting of the High Priest and Virgin. At last, as at first, these two figures fill our mind; their mutual contemplation is compelling. The Virgin is set against the sky, near the top of the stair she is ascending with blithe and childlike confidence, her right hand over her heart. She has no eyes except for the High Priest. She moves up to him without hesitation or drawing back. And he is bent on her entirely. From the height of his great stature, with the supreme majesty of his office about him, the High Priest, between his robe-bearers, extends his hands above the ascending childish figure—a world of thought, of awe, of worship, in that mysterious and lofty benediction.

We will go back again along the Rio della Sensa to the point where we entered it, turning now to the right under the Ponte Rosso into the Rio dei Trasti which soon Widens into a broad way of unbridged water leading out to the lagoon and dividing the island of the Madonna dell' Orto from that of Sant' Alvise. The rio into which we have now come is the third long parallel waterway we have struck in our journey through this district. It stretches on either side of us, spanned by wooden bridges, between the west lagoon and the Sacca della Misericordia. We will follow it for a short distance to the left to the little campo of Sant' Alvise from which it takes its name. Here, in the church hangs that series of strange little canvases that Ruskin did not hesitate to attribute to Carpaccio. They are hung on a wall near the entrance door without order or precaution, signed in great sprawling childish characters Vetor Carpacio. Perhaps our pleasure at penetrating the by-ways of the city to this remote little island makes us at first uncritically appreciative of the quaint square canvases. Ruskin thought them the works of Carpaccio at eight or nine years of age, but he was confessedly writing from memory, and face to face with the reality might have reconsidered his verdict. The paintings seem too sophisticated for a young Carpaccio, too feeble for an older one. The architectural details belong in many respects to a period of the Renaissance later than that which Carpaccio knew, and though, behind their technical incompetence and absurd anachronisms, we seem to catch glimpses of the masterful imaginativeness of Carpaccio, we shall probably feel Molmenti's verdict against their authenticity to be more substantial than Ruskin's reminiscence which was framed in the enthusiasm of his discovery of one of the greatest of Venetian artists. One of the paintings, *The Meeting of Solomon and the Queen of Sheba*, has an interest apart from its quaint fancy. We may conjecture that the artist was drawing on a memory of some work from the east; for the wooden bridge and the figures wavering at each end of it, the winding river, the little round Renaissance building to symbolise Jerusalem, and, above all, the swans in the stream below, and the tall blue peaks in the background, remind us of nothing so much as the willow pattern plate familiar to our childhood. We will leave on one side the scenes from Christ's Passion by Tiepolo, which by some incongruous chance also are preserved in this humble aisleless church, merely remarking that it is necessary to arrive here early; for the sacristan, whose duties extend to both the churches on the two neighbouring islands, hurries off at half-past nine for the office at the Madonna dell' Orto, and Sant' Alvise is shut.

We will return along the rio, past the Madonna dell' Orto and the Palazzo Camello to the Sacca della Misericordia. We shall have occasion elsewhere to speak at length of this unfrequented square of water. It looks out to Murano and the mountains, and is bounded on the south and west by the Abazia della Misericordia and the garden of the Casa degli Spiriti. The Abazia della Misericordia is one of the most beautiful ruins in all Venice. It has its roots far back in the past; for the abbey church was built in 939 and handed over to hermits and, later, to Augustinian Brothers, who added to it a convent. A school was erected beside the church in 1, and this was later enlarged and extended by a hospital and chapel. In the sixteenth century the old hospice was given over to the silk-weavers, and another, more spacious and magnificent, was substituted. On the Fondamenta dell' Abazia, close beside the Scuola di Santa Maria della Misericordia, is a wonderful relief, over the entrance to the hospice for poorer members of the confraternity, bearing the date 1505. It represents the Virgin with robes outspread to enclose and shelter a little company of hooded Brothers who kneel around her; the relief is beautiful in workmanship, and there are traces of lovely colour in the folds of the Virgin's garments. An exquisite square campanile rises in the part of the abbey buildings that is still inhabited by Franciscan Brothers, but the northern front which overlooks the Sacca is a long, roofless, two-storeyed wall of brick with closed shutters—the façade of a weed-grown ruin. This isolated northern wall is exquisite in colouring: its pink plaster has been partly worn away to the red bricks, partly tempered to soft coral where it still lies on the hoary stone. Sparse weeds cover the top, outlined against the sky, and plants which no hand of man has sown spring from the crevices in the brick. In the early morning the Abazia is in shade, and its image in the smooth, shining water is gifted with a new beauty and strength. Looking back upon the east wall, part of which is in ruins, we see the broad Rio di Noale branching in two smaller channels right and left of the garden wall of the police station. This wall has a central window looking out to the lagoon, and often towards evening two figures may be seen through it, framed against the green and taking their pleasure in the garden as in some old picture.

VIEW ON GRAND CANAL.

The Sacca della Misericordia has a majestic corner-stone in the Casa degli Spiriti, the long garden of which is joined to the island of the Abazia by the Ponte della Sacca, a beautiful bridge of pale rose stone bound and lined with white marble. To those who live overlooking the Sacca, the House of the Spirits becomes an inseparable part of the landscape of the lagoon. Modern incredulity has preferred to talk of smugglers instead of spirits, or to find in the weird echoes which inhabit the Sacca and the neighbouring waterways an explanation of its name. Others maintain that it owes it to the companies of wit and intellect that gathered there in the days of Titian and Aretino; no proofs, however, have been offered in support of this alluring suggestion. But if modernity has driven out the spirits, the house itself has become a ghost. In the midst of the thunderstorms which from time to time break over the lagoon the Casa degli Spiriti stands out a ghostly landmark, framed suddenly by a sickle of gold or flashing silver, or illuminated by a level flood of purple, a place of revel for the spirits of the storm. In the calm moonlight it appears more pallid than the moon herself; in the black starless night still the huge corner-stone looms out on the edge of the lagoon. And there is no watch-tower to equal the Casa degli Spiriti for the spectacle of dawn upon the mountains. Those who wake within Venice under a glimmering grey sky, with rifts of remote, transparent blue, hear talk of coming rain. But the House of Spirits which kept watch all night upon the north lagoon, has had its day already in one short hour of dawn. It has seen the Alps rise blue and clear behind the low green line of the mainland; it has seen the ruby fire drawn from them by the dawn; it has seen the crystal path of the lagoon fade to the dove's neck with its waves of peacock green; it has seen the fishing-boats come pressing with their many-coloured sails against the sunrise, each, as it turned before the wind, sealed with a golden blessing from the god of day.

But the House of the Spirits which dominates these, the immaterial glories of the lagoon, rules over a domain of vivid colour and activity. For from the early hours of the morning there is continual traffic down the Sacca of fruit barges bound for Rialto from Sant' Erasmo, the garden of Venice, and of milk barges from the mainland. It is not always an easy life, that of the feeders of the city—in which, as Sansovino says, nothing grows, but everything is found. There are many days when cold and rain and adverse winds mean real suffering to the sellers of fruit and milk. Again and again one is reminded of T. E. Brown's wonderful description of the fishing-boat, with its dirt, its noise, its foul-mouthed crew transformed beneath "the broad benediction of the west" as one sees a milk barge toiling up the channel against wind and tide, with its crowd of men and women. The men begin to hoist the sail with loud excited cries; the women crouch low for shelter, smoking or munching their crusts. They seem lumpish leaden combatants in the lists against the elements, with small hope of conquest. Then, suddenly, as it rounds the corner of the Casa degli Spiriti, the ponderous boat with its dejected crew spreads its sails like a bird, a thing of swift delight lifted into the strong hand of the wind.

If we halt but for an hour in the shadow of the Abazia, we may have a glimpse of many aspects of the city's floating life; joy and mourning follow in unplanned succession, strong passion and the merchandise of every day jostle each other. Now there passes down the Sacca a gondola bearing a coffin to San Michele, now a slow-creeping barge under a mountain of planks, now a little company of lowing calves who can have but one destination in this city without pasture, now a barge of necklaces from Murano that lie coiled together like shining fish of many colours.

There is a moment of late August when all seasons seem to meet and lavish their brightest colours on Rialto, and on the many fruit-stalls of Venice and on the barges that creep leisurely up and down the canals. If we turn again to the heart of the city in the wake of one of those fruit barges, we may imagine ourselves sharing in ancient pomps and festivals. For their tapestry is gorgeous; pyramids of peaches bound about with green leaves, of tomatoes and brilliant pepper pods, huge watermelons cut open to show the crisp, rosy pulp; piles of figs, brown and green; pears, apples, grapes; and choicest of all, the delicious red *fragola* or strawberry-grape. All these and many more make up the brilliant burden of the barges from Sant' Erasmo. We may follow them as they wind through the lesser waterways, now in sun, now in shadow, till the pageant is welcomed in the full flowing day of the Grand Canal and the barges empty themselves at Rialto.

Chapter Ten
ARTISTS OF THE VENETIAN RENAISSANCE

IT can be no matter for wonder that colour was the elected medium of expression for Venice: endowed, by reason of her water, with a twofold gift of light, she was also perhaps more splendid than any other city in the details of her daily life. Colour was its substance. Everything was pictorial and rich and festive. Even on a dark day the rooms of the Accademia seem full of sunshine from the treasure they hold of ancient Venice. If Bellini's *Procession of the Cross* on the Piazza of San Marco were missing from its place, we should feel that a light had been put out. The Venetians had always been decorators. The pictures of the first masters—Vivarini, d'Alemagna, Jacobello del Fiore and many others—seem literally spun out of the furnaces of Murano. They are no primitives in their mastery of colour. Consider for a moment the *Madonna and Saints* of Vivarini and d'Alemagna in the Sala della Presentazione. The natural life of the fields has been made to serve a design of amazing richness. The Virgin's golden throne is carved With acorns and roses, and luxuriant oak foliage forms its decorative fringe; the fruits of the garden in which she sits are lavished round her; the grass is gemmed with countless tiny flowers, trefoil and strawberry, milkwort and potentilla, and the infant Christ has burst open a golden pomegranate, displaying its burden of rich crimson seeds. There is scarcely a harmony of colour unattempted, scarcely a jewel unset, from the rainbow of the angels' wings, and the rim of fluctuating colours on the Virgin's green robe folded back over peacock blue, to the mosaics in the burning gold of the angels' haloes, in the Virgin's crown, and in the mitres of the Fathers. There too is the very vermilion of Veronese, that wonderful salvia scarlet to which the *Feast in Levi's House* owes so much of its decorative significance. We shall be better equipped for understanding the early colour-masters if we realise that their dowry came to them not only from the lagoon. The marvellous rainbow of Venice the "Ambiguous One" was not their only light nor the deep azure and emerald and gold, which she hung about her, the only jewels they knew. The garment of Venetian art is inwoven with threads of mountain glory, of rich harvests of grape and golden grain: we must go up into the mainland of Venice to understand the art of the first masters no less than that of Giorgione, Titian, Tintoretto and Veronese, whose conceptions were penetrated with the very sunshine of earth, a warmer-bodied, fuller sunshine than Venice of the waters could know, full of secret throbbings of the hidden springing life for light and ripening. Autumn is the loom on which was woven the robe of Venetian art, autumn with its indomitable splendours of gold and silver, green and cremoisin and the supreme scarlet of the salvia. These colours are steeped in an impermeable dye: they seem saturated with the light, burning out the more gloriously, the more intensely, as their allotted span grows less. The passion of the spring is of another kind; it needs the present magic of the sun to draw out its exquisite, incipient radiance; it cannot lavish glory except when his countenance is bent upon it. But in the radiance of autumn foliage there is a daring that darkness is impotent to quell: it is like a shout of triumph in the face of death, a procession of all the glory of earth into the kingdom of the dead, not reluctant, not made fearful by the rumours that have floated to it in the grey-mantled dawn, in the fierce trumpeting of rain and wind; boldly, gloriously it marches, scattering joyfully the gems it cannot hold, that nothing shall be saved. We sing no dirge, but a triumph song, as the golden trophies fall—a gold more refulgent than Bellini's façade of San Marco, though this was gold of the purest even Venice, the golden city, could win from her furnaces. We may still see these mainland autumns where the colour-masters gathered their treasures; on the borders of the mountains we may sit in such a garden of the Madonna as Vivarini and his fellows record. In the late autumn the sun is slow to win his way; but when he comes there is no splendour to rival the fire of the salvia-beds, round cups of concentrated light springing up into spires and tongues of flame among the arrow-shaped green leaves. No words can describe the brilliance of this leaping flame, devouring the sunshine like fuel, and scattering it abroad in myriad gems of penetrating brightness. In the long luminous grass of the lawn will be scattered here and there a rose-bush of the Madonna's crimson, and tall gold-edged lilies may be seen through the close-hung flaps of the medusa leaves. This splendid tapestry is spread upon a poplar background of flickering gold and green, the steadier gold of low mulberries, and grey-bodied autumn apple-trees on which the leaves glow blood-red, while behind all rise the grassy slopes of the mountain outposts crossed by the shadow of some jutting rock.

Often among the humbler Venetian painters, less versed in the deeper significance of human life and religious symbol, we find a singular mastery of perspective and many signs of familiarity with the interplay of light and shade among the mountains. We are reminded again and again of their apprenticeship to nature as we see one of the countless ruined towers on the outposts of the Alps rising against the golden sunset light within its threadbare rampart of dusky branches. The face of the mountains was a vital and intimate fact to them, not an accepted piety. We are, for instance, often tempted to consider the persons of Cima's sacred themes less as the essential interest than as a finely designed harmony of colour in the foreground of a landscape. In his native city of Conegliano he stored his mind with mountain wonders, and in his wide and delicate horizons there are many touches inspired by a living memory of the scene. We have known the joy of that limpid atmosphere after days of mist and rain, those floating sunlit clouds upon the transparent blue, that jewel-like gleam of a deep pool, the delicacy of autumn trees passing into gold, the foretaste of an untrodden stronghold in the winding paths that lose themselves and come again to view as they coil up the castled heights. The landscape is conventionalised of course, but its spirit is there—its rare shades of colour, its marvellous varieties of depth; and ever behind, there is the vision of the mountains cutting into the sky in a sharp, clear, azure coldness, or with a luminous haze round their base in the mellowness of an autumn day. As backgrounds we see them only, for Venice had other needs than of mountains; but many of these painters knew them as near realities; they had stept home in the glory of an autumn sunset amid the revel of the vintage, their whole being intoxicated with the wine and the splendour of life; they had drunk that fresh-trodden, unfermented juice, the *vino mosto*, sufficient to stir those whose senses are alert and in whom the passion of the world runs high. It needed indeed a Titian to transform the vintage of Cadore into the bacchic rout of his *Ariadne*, but it is there, in the wooded mountain slopes, in the pageantry of evening, when the fancy soars to Ariadne's crown faintly dawning in the warm blue, and sweeps round some mist-clad inland lake to float among the turreted heights.

PALAZZO REZZONICO.

Or if we take our stand on the keep of the ruined Roman citadel of Asolo, when the evening light streaming down into the shadowy undulations of the valley, which tosses in ceaseless waves round the mountain's base, illuminates a land of rich and golden peace, we feel again the painters of Venice at our side; the vague, rich spirit of the winding valleys, allied with the solemn grandeur of the mountains, above whose dark barrier we have glimpses of remote and shining peaks, the tiny citadels half gathered into the folding mist, the alternate radiance and keen obscurity of the lower peaks now visited and now forsaken by the inconstant sunset light, the sudden illumination of a solitary peasant or a single tree in sharp relief against the twilight—all these have passed into the canvas of Giorgione: in him, above all, we seem to drink that wondrous potion compact of evening vapour and golden light which the sunset pours into the dim goblet of the mountain valleys. And we may record here, how, in the last period of the Venetian Renaissance, the great decorator Veronese found a field of activity under the shadow of Asolo. When Marcantonio Barbaro, Procurator of San Marco, and his brother the Patriarch of Aquileja, bade Palladio build their villa at the little village of Maser, they called on their friend Paolo to decorate it within. And this perfect villa is one of the happiest monuments to the two artists; the excellent skill of both is brought into congenial play, and to the courtly old patrician Barbaro we owe a debt which perhaps we partly cancel in the coin of our pleasure. The simple yet sumptuous villa lies so dexterously disposed below its cypress hill, that it seems almost to consist of the loggia alone as we climb up the garden slope from the road, through the judicious mingling of smooth lawn and scythe-cut grass full of scabious and delicate Alpine flowers. Delicious scents float down from the late roses along the terrace and the brilliant flower-beds in the grass; the medusa tree stands luminous against the evergreen shrubs and cypress, and against the yellow wall a huge cactus raises its mysterious purple sword-blade. The villa is spacious and full of air and light; the suite of rooms above the loggia, containing the great part of Paolo's work, open one out of the other, and each has a glass door that leads directly to the lawn and grotto in the cleft of the hill behind, while the central hall lies open on each side to wide stretches of mountain country. There were no stern censors here to ask Paolo if his homely details were quite in keeping with the gravity of his theme; the artist was working for a friend in a house that was full of light and sunshine and the clear mountain air, and he has put his soul with most lucid fantasy into the allegories of autumn and springtime, of Cybele and Juno, Vulcan and Apollo, of dogs and boys and girls at play among the mimic balconies, of sprays of fig and vine leaf; into the figures of Michelangelesque strength reclining above the doors, and the tiny processions of men and beasts in chiaroscuro on the friezes; into the clear, radiant faces of women and sinewy forms of men; the eloquent dogs and lions; and not least into the lithe and gallant figure of himself, advancing from the mimic door at one end of the long vista to meet the lady who trips out from the opposite end, *l'amica dell' artista*—or, as the guide-book discreetly says—his wife. The portrait of himself is done with much imagination and even pathos. He was a dreamer, too, this Veronese. These figures of the painter and his dog give us pause; they make us feel that he would have been good to walk the mountains with; that if he could step out now from the room where he keeps continual watch, on to the exquisite grass plot, with its happy tuft of white anemone and pale Michaelmas daisy, we might win from him some mountain confidence which he has not entrusted to canvas or fresco. It is a pleasure to picture Veronese at his work upon Marcantonio's villa. Every midday he must have had good progress to show; for these blithe works that have kept their colour so fresh and strong are executed with a few brave master strokes: they are no less potent in their swift presentment than in their conception. We can see him dismounting from his scaffold at the summons of Barbaro, returned from his morning round among his stables or his orchards; we can see him still keen and stirred by the creative impulse, full of that excited pleasure which accompanies expression, standing a little aside while Barbaro bears his admiration to and fro—now confessing that time and office have rusted his mythology and asking the meaning of some emblem; now on the lookout for a freak of his friend, some beast or bird put in perhaps to give him joy; now in raptures over the old shoes and broom, which he swears he has just thrashed the maid for leaving on the cornice, while Paolo stands by brimming with mirth at the deception; now called upon to guess the significance of the fair lady bridled by her lord, which the guide-book ungallantly interprets as the victory of virtue over vice, but which to Marcantonio no doubt seemed capable of less abstract explanation. With all their nobility of design and execution, there is something about these frescoes so intimate and sympathetic as to impart to us the actual joy and health of spirit which conceived them. Given the skill and the robust and prodigal genius of Veronese, how should they not be joyous in these halls full of light and air and sunshine, the song of birds and of trickling water, the sounds of meadow and mountain. We may take leave of the mountains in the midst of one of those brave companies which must often have gathered in this earthly Paradise of Marcantonio Barbaro round the long table spread in the loggia—such a loggia as Paolo himself so often painted—looking out, through the arches to the vista of creepered wall and over the green meadows studded with golden fruit-trees, to the undulating country and tracts of woodland, now bathed in liquid sunshine, now gathered into a soft-enfolding haze—a wide ocean from which the campaniles rise like masts of ships, and over which the distant villas are scattered like shining fishing-boats.

"These workmen," says d'Annunzio of the Venetian artists of the Renaissance, "create in a medium that is itself a joyous mystery—in colour, the ornament of the world, in colour, which seems to be the striving of the spirit to become light. And the entirely new, musical understanding they have of colour acts in such a way that their creation transcends the narrow limits of the symbols it represents and assumes the lofty, revealing faculty of an infinite harmony." Colour—which seems to be the striving of the spirit to become light. These words recur to us again and again face to face with the Venetian masters. By the primitives the colours are laid on as accessory to the scene, as it were fine enamel; in the Renaissance painters, they are not only woven into the fabric of the picture, it grows and moves through them. We may choose, in illustration, Giovanni Bellini's small picture of the *Madonna with St. Catherine and the Magdalen* in the Accademia, because, though it is in one sense less completely representative of the distinguishing features of the Venetian school than, for instance, his masterpiece of the *Frari*, it realises perhaps more fully than any that "new and musical understanding of colour" which was the peculiar gift of the Venetians. It is literally informed with radiance; flesh itself has become spirit, no longer a covering, but an atmosphere—a directly perfect expression. There is no denial or emaciation of the flesh; the forms are strong, the habitations of a potent earth-spirit. The faces are pondering, penetrating, profound, and withal extremely individual; they might seem impassive, were it not that every feature is kindled by the pervading colour till we seem to feel it as a sensuous presence. It is a quality of colour that so subtly determines the poise of their hands, that makes their touch so sensitively penetrating that feeling seems to flow from it without pressure. The solemn harmony of red and green and blue, and of the diffused radiance of the flesh tints, is not only lit from without by the sunlight, it seems literally to burn from within, depth behind depth, with light.

The peculiarly luminous treatment of the flesh perfected by Bellini in repose, it remained for Tintoretto to realise in motion; this we may venture to illustrate from a work too immense for our discussion in any but a limited aspect—his last great work, *The Paradise*, in the Ducal Palace. The quality we are seeking in it becomes the more remarkable on account of its loss of superficial colour, so that at first it seems cold and faded as if a mist had fallen upon it; then, very slowly, like day breaking out of the veil, colour reveals itself as a fresh property in the forms. We cannot penetrate the depth of it; rank behind rank the luminous faces define themselves like mysterious shapes of the atmosphere, some mere ghosts in the depths which daylight cannot pierce, some radiant already with the light; and across and through them all, through the flame-winged throng of Cherubim, piercing all companies and ranks of being to the extremes of the vast canvas, shoot the rays from the central source of light in the seat of Christ. It is a symphony of colour become almost vocal; we perceive it not only with the eye but in all our senses, this music of the spheres which one man has dared to gather into a single canvas. Who but Tintoretto could have dreamed of achieving this perspective built solely of human forms and faces? Into all the mysteries of life—those echoes of experience which we touch but faintly, those substances with which we feel inexplicable correspondencies—into these Tintoretto has looked: the rays from behind the Son of God have poured into the heart of the universe, and from it has grown his Paradise. Joy is the heart of this great symphony; it works upon us rather as a creative force than as a thing created, sounding continually some new note or rarer harmony of colour. At times it overpowers us, and then amid the maze of divine musicians and Cherubim and Seraphim and Thrones and Principalities and Powers, some single harmonious human form, strong in beauty, with wings of light, some tender, lovely face of youth or woman, the solemn gesture of saint or bishop, the rainbow of an angel's wing, gives our intellect a resting-place. For it is not through obscuring of outlines that this wonder of music in colour is accomplished; the human form, on which all the notes are played, is become indeed a perfect instrument, but not by forfeiting its material strength or substance; the structure is massive, solid—if to our notion of solidity we may unite the gift of perfect ease within an element whose progress only is by flight, where each moment is poised but slightly in its passage to the next, where there is no time because no stable unit to serve as pedestal for time. In this great picture, that faculty of the Venetian painters which we are now illustrating, found perhaps its completest realisation—the power of winging flesh with colour so that it is endowed with the very properties of atmosphere.

By permission of Arnold Mitchell, Esq.

TOWARDS THE RIALTO, SAN ANGELO.

This luminous quality of the Venetian painters is realised by them in many more general ways than in the treatment of the human form. We may consider it in Carpaccio in relation to the significance of landscape in his compositions. It is his power of treating a scene atmospherically that supplies one chief charm of his work. It is never on a day of splendour that either he or Gentile Bellini depicts Venice; but constantly on a cold, colourless day of late autumn the waters of Carpaccio seem to live again for us as we have seen them through the perspective of his arches or in the background of a city picture. We may see the Grand Canal wind into the dark city under the pale familiar gold of his Rialto sunset, and scattered sails on the cold, clear lagoon in weird contrast of orange with the steely waters or with the pale rose or white of buildings. There is a peculiar fascination in this clear neutrality of light in sky and water and buildings; it is no less a property of Venice than her more refulgent harmonies. Whatever hour of day it comes, it has the strange revelation of the dawn about it, a curious remoteness in which the works of men arrest attention as if fraught with a new purport. The emotional significance of landscape was understood by Carpaccio in a wonderful degree. How much depends, for instance, in the scene where Ursula's father dismisses the English ambassadors, on the vista of canal across which lights fall from dividing waterways! It is the narrowest strip; but the sunlight on the houses, the exquisite arch of pale blue sky fading into white above the distant buildings, give a new value to the interior; the outside world, on which the sun is shining, seems to look into the room with the streaming light. A still more beautiful illustration of Carpaccio's understanding of light is to be found in the room where St. Ursula lies asleep. It seems, in fact, scarcely an indoor room; through its open doors and windows it is in close touch with the air and sky; and the effect of contact with wind and sky is heightened by the real plumage of the angel's grey wings, while the back-sweep of his robe suggests a sudden alighting after flight with the current of air still about him. We know of no picture to surpass this of Carpaccio in conveying the atmosphere of a room into which the first light is breaking— the exhilaration of an illumined wall, the waking of colour on window-ledge, chair and bedcover, the blending of luminous and shadowy. It is the light of the first dawn, the infancy of day, with a suggestion of unillumined sky, just creeping out of shadow in the expanse of open, untrellised window behind the plants, a soft, wonderful stealing green, that has not yet come into its kingdom. Even buildings are made by Carpaccio to serve an atmospheric effect. We might illustrate from almost every picture in San Giorgio degli Schiavoni, but confining ourselves to the St. Ursula series, we shall find a notable illustration in the buildings seen through the water-gate in the *Return of the Embassy*, and in the great Renaissance loggia which fills so conspicuous a place in the foreground, and to which airiness and light have been imparted by its great arches, by the water washing round its base, and by the spring of the bridge that connects it with the campo where the King sits under his canopy. Most striking of all, perhaps, is the subtle architectural treatment by which, in the great threefold scene of the Prince's departure, his meeting with Ursula and their blessing by the King, Carpaccio has bestowed an atmosphere of remoteness, almost of fairy strangeness on the English harbour with its castles and walls and motley buildings soaring far up the rocky hillside into the sky, an atmosphere entirely distinct from the upper-world light and joyousness of the contrasting court of Ursula's father.

There is an element of his native landscape that Carpaccio incorporated with singular felicity, and which is peculiarly prominent in his pictures—namely the shipping of Venice. In the great trilogy of the Prince's departure the vessels are a masterpiece: there is nothing to surpass them in this kind. Carpaccio seems to have realised to the full their varied elements of beauty: their static properties, their weight and substance and the symmetry of their frame, combined with all the radiant light and spring of swelling sail and rigging and flag and countless trappings: all that goes to make a sailing ship a thing of music. And it is not only vessels rigged and ready to float in triumph on the high seas that Carpaccio depicts: there is a vessel also *in squero*, with all the song gone from it, one might think, lying uneasily on its side with its huge mast aslant across the harbour tower. It is noteworthy that all the vessels of the English King seem in course of repair; there is something in their semi-skeleton condition which singularly reinforces the dream effect that we have noticed in this portion of the picture, and the triumphant vessel that would seem to belong to the gay town on our right is united in feeling to the shadow city on the left by the exceeding mystery and beauty of its reflection. This picture supplies us with another instance of the way in which Venice operated as an inspiration in the work of Carpaccio, even when he was not directly portraying the city itself. The beautiful effect of a drawbridge over a great water, such as he knew familiarly in Venice, had impressed itself on his mind: adapting it to the requirements of his scene, he reproduces the bridge of Rialto in the city of the English King, not forgetting the significance of a crowning figure in white at the apex of the arch. We cannot indeed afford to miss a detail in Carpaccio: there is never any crowding nor taking refuge in vagueness. The varieties of shipping, the flags hung from the windows, the most distant figures, are all treated with the same clearness and precision: to each its value is assigned. This fulness of meaning is one of the sources of his fascination for us: the fact that he has done a little thing means sometimes more to us, if we can come at the prompting purpose, than a pageant of main figures. It is like the side-flash of light which a seemingly irrelevant act casts sometimes on a personality.

The fidelity of Bellini and Carpaccio to the facts of Venice fills us continually with fresh wonder: it is not the fidelity of copyists standing outside the scene they paint; their very heart is in its stones. As we watch Gentile's gorgeous procession sweep like a stream from the gate of the Ducal Palace round the border of the Piazza, with the sound of trumpets, the rustle and swing of noble garments and the gleam of banners, we feel that the painter had heard and felt the triumph of the music, so marvellously has he conveyed its influence in these moving figures; we too hear the jubilation of it as the long tubes pass out and in. With the pictures of Carpaccio and Gentile Bellini before us we may do more than conjecture what manner of men they were who filled the foreground of contemporary Venice. We have not masses or dispositions of colour merely: we seem to move through a crowd of living beings or a gallery of portraits. No one could paint loungers as Carpaccio paints them; there is no monotony in their inaction; the faces are as various as the men—wonderful faces, some coarse, some refined, but almost all with that indefinable quality of pathos in their strength which is one of the essentials of beauty. There are perhaps comparatively few among them that would satisfy a conventional canon of beauty: their fascination lies in the rich combination of whimsical humour and strength, melancholy and wit; so eloquent are they, so quick with intelligence that we are little disposed to question their material perfection or imperfection. These citizens of Gentile Bellini, Mansueti and above all Carpaccio—since in him are realised a far greater variety of types—impress us profoundly as men of calm and steady purpose, who have lived, felt and prevailed. They are men of action, yet they are dreamers. And this was not from incapacity in Carpaccio to express vivid motions in feature or form. When he is more freely composing, as in the *Death of St. Ursula*, it would be hard to rival the brilliance and vivacity with which he has treated the turmoil of the one-sided fray. But these citizens—whether of Venice or of Ursula's court is immaterial—seem to be governed by some internal harmony; there is a rhythm in their motions and in their standing still, which reflects the spirit of their time. We have only to compare them with the characters in Longhi's eighteenth-century interiors to understand that a great change has taken place. Imagine Carpaccio and Bellini set to paint as primary interests the choosing of a dress, the stopping of a tooth, the guessing of a riddle, a dancing lesson, a toilette. These things were part of life, and superbly they would have done it; they painted lesser acts than these in the corner of their pictures, for every detail of the city life so jealously guarded by its rulers was precious to them. But the difference lies in the centre of interest. In the eighteenth century, the detail, the side light, the accessory of life has swelled into the principal subject, and the faces of the actors are vacant as never in Carpaccio. It is not so much that they are less beautiful, that they are often witless; but they are lacking in purpose, in subordination to a common control. The pulse of a great civic life no longer beats in them.

We have considered hitherto the manner in which Venice used her elected medium of expression, how her painters had understood and interpreted the life of the city. We will turn now to ask what attitude towards the facts of life is reflected in their canvases. And here we will attempt again to illustrate, by certain examples, what aspects of life found most ready acceptance by the Venetian artists of the Renaissance. We may venture to seek an illustration of two of its broader aspects— one foreign, the other native to the mind of Venice as reflected in her life and in her art—in two sculptured figures by Antonio Rizzo in the courtyard of the Ducal Palace. These two figures, of Adam and Mars, are most original in conception. Adam holds the apple in his hand; it seems that he has just partaken of it and that, partaking, he has been initiated into a new vision. His beautiful clear-cut face is upturned; his lips are open; his hand seems to hold in the tumult of his heart. There is as yet no shame, no contrition, no sense of sin in Adam's look, nor in his attitude, but the immense wonder of a new experience with its yet undetermined import; and through the ecstasy of his vision there breaks that strange pain of the mortal man whose body can scarcely support its spiritual burden. It seems almost as if Adam were receiving now that vision of the ages at whose threshold he stood; he has opened a door which can never again be shut; he has let in a flood which is beyond his control, and he is rapt in the contemplation. The other figure who fills with Adam a niche in the Arco Foscari is Mars, the god of war. His body is grandly moulded, stalwart and disciplined and ready for action; but there are no tempests in his look; there is no herculean development of muscle nor trampling vehemence as in the fresco of Veronese. Rizzo's war-god is young, full of grace and beauty, with the dream also of a poet on his sensuous lips. He is majestic; his face is grave and thoughtful, with a strange sadness in its vigilant wisdom. He and Adam seem to strike together the accord of the Renaissance, the union of a great expectancy, an uncomprehended newness, with controlled and ordered purpose and the conviction of conquest. It is the latter aspect which seems to find reflection in the mind of Venice not the mystic promise, the troubled vision, which the Renaissance held for some of those on whom its influence fell. In the Venetians of the first Renaissance there is always the note of calm and assured knowledge; we may find it again and again in their artistic annals. In the Casa Civran—the so-called Casa dell' Otello beside the Campo dei Carmini—we again recognise Rizzo's hand in one of the most lovely and characteristic figures of the first Renaissance, which has fortunately survived the various restorations and spoliations of the house and stands still intact in its lonely niche on the plastered wall. It is impossible to convey in words the vivacity, the nobility and grace of this young warrior: the proud and magnificent control governing each motion of his spirited form, the rhythm in response to which each member of him moves, so that the effect on us is indeed that of a song, a victorious, joyful melody. Again and again we may meet them, Mars and his young disciple, and others of their kin, in Carpaccio's crowds. The young Civran warrior might have stept on to his niche from the *Death of St. Ursula*; moreover, the life that thrills in him is felt not in single figures only, but in the entire conception of series after series of Carpaccio, in Bellini's *Procession of the Cross*, in Tintoretto's *St. Ursula and the Virgins* in the Church of the Mendicanti.

It was thus the Venetians confronted life. In portrait, allegory or story, realised in varying degrees of naïvety, splendour and refinement, with more or less penetration and psychological insight, we find the same balance and control—a unique harmony of strength, grace and serenity. And if we turn to the religious art of Venice we shall be struck by a lack of anything like mystic rapture or absorption in the sufferings of Christ. We have but two examples in Venice of Bellini's portrayal of the facts of Christ's mature life, but he has treated the theme of the Madonna and Child with a unique profundity. The mystery of life seems to be shadowed in the face of his Madonnas; his saints and apostles, so striking in their individuality, so virile in their piety, have a significance beyond their perfect act of worship. No Venetian religious painter before Tintoretto equalled Bellini in solemnity and depth of conception; but in all we find the same pervading calm, the same absence of tumult or the disturbing element of pain or agony. We will choose an example from Basaiti—the most perfect, perhaps, of all his works—in illustration of what seems to us a prevailing characteristic of the Venetian mind both for strength and weakness—his *Gesu morto con due Angeli*. It is striking in its originality of conception and full of noble and tender sentiment. There are no weeping women, no agonised apostles round the body of Jesus; only the very young keep watch beside him, two winged infants, at his head and at his feet. They have found him here, this young dead god, laid out as if asleep upon the flat stone by the rock—no blasted rock, its crags are covered with living shrubs and plants. And he is in the light: there is no ghostly pallor in his face upturned to the sky, upon his long, dark hair; so beautiful a brow, such tender cheeks, so strong and brave a neck they have never seen. And he is so still, he lies without fear, not heeding them. They must not wake him from his sleep. The infant at his head, whose exquisitely moulded face is full of that strangely pathetic, antique wisdom of the very young, half-elfish, half-infantile, feels the burden of his sagacity upon him. Why had that brow a crown of thorns instead of flowers about it? This youth to whom they will now bear company had not chosen well his pillow or his crown—though he is so beautiful he was not wise enough to know that thorns are not for those who would be at rest. In the picture the wise infant has taken off the prickly crown that it may not pierce and rend the dream that holds the sleeper there so long; he is full of the knowledge of his triumph, half-fearful lest it should not be complete. The crown of thorns hangs on his own left arm, which he raises half in warning, half in wonder, feeling as his elbow bends the thorns upwards on his arm from what pain he has saved that beautiful but foolish youth. And with his right hand he fondles the hair of Jesus, drawing it a little back from his forehead to be sure that in his stealthy theft he has not left some scratch, some mark of pain. But there are no traces of the crown in any sign of pain, only a faint, faint band beneath the hair he has drawn back—a shadow, as it were, of Christ's regality. *He saved others, Himself He cannot save.* Now with this little Saviour, this guardian of his pillow, he can at last sleep in peace. The infant at the feet is more babylike, less wise, more gleefully wondering. He has found no thorns on that beautiful, still body, but he has found another wonder at the feet. The toes of one he holds in his tiny hand, stroking it in his delight: he has found, it seems, a little hole upon the instep bone that the feet of humans are not wont to wear, and he points in musing, half-delighted wonder to the other foot, where he spies the same strange mark. It is a game to this curly headed cherub. He has not yet dreamed of contact with something beyond the reach of his baby wisdom. There is not yet in his chubby face that look which has stolen into the face of his brother and which now seems to put a world between them, a look that amid all its elfish aloofness is akin to the solicitude of human love. What dream was this of Basaiti—the figure of this young God of Light—perfect in form, luminous and strong, unspoiled and untroubled in his sleep of death? His eyes if they were open would be fountains fed from the beauty of the world, but he has borne no burden of humanity. There is power to suffer in that strong and beautiful young face, but it is not the power of the Man of Sorrows. This is not Jesus who agonised in the garden, or who wrote upon the ground; it is not the man from whom Pilate turned away his face.

BRONZE WELL-HEAD BY ALBERGHETTI,
COURTYARD OF PALAZZO DUCALE.

There is one only—the last and greatest of the Venetians of
the Renaissance—who could sound all notes of tragedy and
pathos as well as notes of joy. Tintoretto, the supreme
Venetian, the greatest exponent of the essential spirit of
Venice, is the son of a wider kingdom than hers and of a greater
age than the Renaissance. Unsurpassed as designer and
colourist, he is endowed throughout with the peculiar gifts of
Venice; but during those years of passionate study, in which he
was winning here and there the secrets of his art, hungry for
knowledge, careless of gain, and bargaining only for material in
which to realise his conceptions—during those years in which
he lived alone in continual meditation on some fresh labour,
he was probing the deep and passionate things of humanity as
no Venetian artist had ever probed them before. The streets
and churches of the city seem to echo still to the steps of this
genius at once so robust, so tender, so profound and so joyous.
Ridolfi laments the lavishness of his production, arguing that
restraint of his overflowing fantasy would have strengthened
his conceptions. But Tintoretto had to work in his own way;
the instinct that flowered in the Scuola di San Rocco, the

Bacchus and Ariadne and the *Paradiso*, might be trusted to choose the manner of its relaxation as well as of its labour. No painter, perhaps, has so wonderfully combined the dramatist and lyrist; for Tintoretto with all his vast imaginative strength had power also over the tenderest springs of melody. There is hardly a picture of his in which some exquisite face of youth or woman will not strike a note of tenderness, and we need only call to mind the *Visitation* in the Scuola di San Rocco, to know what Tintoretto's tenderness could be. He had that power, the gift only of the greatest, so intensely to imagine his central theme that the most perfectly executed and conspicuous detail does not divert us into lesser issues. It is exactly here that his distinguishing greatness reveals itself He is completely sincere. His vision is too comprehensive to overlook what really filled the foreground; his skill of hand too great to allow its inclusion to be other than an element in the realisation of his central theme; his concentration too intense to make him fear lest an accessory should become a primary interest. We may pause for a moment in consideration of his greatest tragic triumph, the *Crucifixion*, in the Scuola di San Rocco. The theme is immense, and, like the *Death of Abel*, it is treated in a great elemental spirit. Amid all the throes of nature and the sufferings of the Son of Man, the world goes on its way. The ghostly figure of the Arab on his camel, and the caravan winding down from the city to depart into the desert, the two splendid knights who gaze without pity or understanding on this spectacle of the death of slaves, the man who leans from his donkey behind the Cross of Christ, all are as prominent to their little circle as they would be in life; and they have just that prominence for us—the immediate participators in the tragedy—that they would have in life. As always in Tintoretto, the horizon is vast. Wide ranges of blue, undulating country extend to the mountains, above which breaks his peculiar, tender, yellow light of dawn; he has made them recede into unimagined distance by setting across the mountains and the light the raised arm of a mounted figure. There is a great calm in this horizon, while in the middle distance above the Arab the wind has set the leaves quivering on a tree whose thin and twisted branches sway wildly against the blackness of the storm. The most impressive light for this picture is obtained when the setting sun illuminates the marvellous group of mourners at the foot of the Cross, so that they stand out in startling brightness against the heightened depths of the vast background, while Christ hangs above them dark within the darkness.

EVENING IN THE PIAZZETTA.

The Scuola di San Rocco is the supreme monument to Tintoretto's poetic, as to his plastic genius. If we are justified in feeling that his understanding of the life of Christ may be a true touchstone of a man's philosophy, it will become a matter of first interest to us to know how so profound a thinker as Tintoretto approached the subject. There is no lack here indeed of tragic depth. *The Temptation of Christ* is sufficient alone to vindicate Tintoretto as gifted with understanding above his fellows. Another might have compassed the tumultuous, beautiful earth-spirit, with muscular, proud, uplifted arms, and face burning with desire; but who else could have added that touch of impotence to his restless, aspiring gesture, or have dreamed the tenderness in the lovely, sorrowful face of Christ that looks down on this radiant creature of desire, entirely without judgment or stern denial, but as if too remote from the appeal to make reply? The exceeding pathos of this picture would have been missed if Lucifer, the brightest of the spirits that fell, were a whit less radiant; if Christ's face had one shade less of compassion in its wondering aloofness. And for our last example we may choose a picture in which the strength of Tintoretto is realised in quietness so complete that a hush seems to lie about it. No painting of his is greater in conception than that of *Christ before Pilate*. The moment he has chosen is that in which Pilate performs his vain ablution before the multitude who lightly accept the guilt he attempts to transfer, in the awful cry, "His blood be on us and on our children." Tintoretto has set Pilate's face in shadow: a single ray falls across the pillar behind his head. He looks away from Christ but not towards the crowd: he has spoken: he would fain make an end of this drama. It is the fine, thoughtful, astute face of a Venetian councillor that Tintoretto has depicted. Christ stands before him in the full light—removed only by a single step—a motionless white figure above the restless crowd, complete in control, gathered into himself and folded in a great silence and calm; yet not now more alone than when the crowds cried after him day and night for a sign. His head is bowed upon his breast: his closely folded robe follows the slight curve of his body: his bound hands lie nerveless in their cords: yet beside the strength of this bound prisoner the animation of the foreground figure who grips the cord is impotence indeed. Most wonderful of all perhaps is the contrast of a busy scribe at his table below the judgment-seat, pausing with suspended pen for the words that shall convict, with the majestic, motionless figure of Christ. We seem to hear the words proceeding from those closed lips: he would utter them so, not moving. It is less the originality of this picture that impresses us than its profound directness and truth, comparable only to the story it illustrates. In understanding none has surpassed the conception of that single, solitary figure, face to face with the vast fabric of the judgment-hall, weighted with its burden of custom and tradition; none has more profoundly imagined the tragic triumph in that entire loneliness of the great and good before the tribunal of man.

Chapter Eleven
THE SOUL THAT ENDURES

ON an evening of late September Venice revealed herself to one of her lovers amidst a spectacle beyond any range of dreams. Evening was closing in upon the city with cloud and breeze. In the church of San Giorgio Maggiore the Tintorettos gleamed dimly from the walls; daylight was gone. But in the tower high overhead, clear of the shadows of confining buildings, the day had still a course to run. The tide was low, and land and water stretched out in interchanging coils of olive and azure beneath a purple storm-cloud, whilst ever against the bar of the Lido rolled the sea, dyed with that celestial blue that sometimes steals from the Adriatic into the basin of San Marco to prostrate itself at the conquering Lion's feet. And there lay Venice, her form outlined against a flood of pearl, the water bending in a tender, luminous bow behind her towers. Far away, across the mysterious expanse of low lagoon, Torcello and Burano gleamed out in startling pallor against the storm, amid a wild confusion of dark earth and glittering water. The Northern Alps were hidden in darkness at the horizon, but westward across the mainland the clear, sharp peaks of the Euganean hills rose up behind the city's pearly halo, behind the deep blue of the surging lowlands, in almost unearthly outline against the sunset sky. In front of them a livid fire rolled sullenly along the valley, sending up purple smoke into the cloud. The storm genie, summoned by nether powers, was descending to his fearful tryst behind the Euganeans, but, as he sank, he bent his face upon the pale form of Venice, his enchantress, and the fire of his wonder and of his adoration kindled in all her slumbering limbs a glow of responsive life. A flood of crimson suffused the pallor of her pearly diadem, and her maidens, sleeping grey among the waters round her, unfolded rosy petals upon the surface of the lagoon.

It is this power of living communion with the daily pageant in which sun and moon are doge and emperor, and the stars and the clouds their retinue—this it is which, finding expression once at Venice in a temporal glory that has passed away, is the abiding assurance of her immortality. This is the spirit which, if once it helped to make her great, still makes her great to-day, the spirit that endures. For Venice is not a dead body: she is a living soul. Overflowing all moulds in which we may think to contain her, she reveals herself continually in new mystery, new wonder. We spoke of Venice as being paved with sky, and every day there is cast upon her pavement a fresh revelation of changefulness and beauty. A thousand forms and patterns move in procession over the water, passing each instant into something "rich and strange," a fleeting succession of aerial designs drawn with tremulous pencil in colours which never lived on the palette of a mortal artist. There is a body of truth at the root of the old fancy which gifted water-maidens with subtler, more perilously powerful allurements than their sisters of the land. Their element is mutability, but they are not soulless, as men have said: it is only that their soul is as the soul of water—luminous, flowing, mutable, reflective, musical, profound: for, though they are mutable, they are not shallow; it is a part of their being that they should be susceptible of change. They cannot tire their victims, they whose beauty is continually renewed; and yet it may be that men do well to fear them, for they have secret communings with things men do not dream of. Venice has held men, she holds them still, with the fascination of a water spirit; they yield to her, they grasp her, but she is still before them, never mastered, never fully known. Let those for whom conquest is the ideal in love beware of Venice the incomparable, the uncompassable: they who would win her must have power to worship what they cannot comprehend, they must desire to leave her spirit free. Then she will unfold her heart to them, she will give herself in a moment when the pursuit is still. And to those who can receive the gift, she will give herself again and yet again; only they must come freshly expectant of each fresh revelation, not clinging to past impressions, not claiming a memory to be revived. For each renewal is a transformation, and we must bring new senses to receive it, senses alive and fresh as earth each morning to the touch of the old sun ever new.

Venice, when she was most glorious, did but catch and imprison in her stones those matchless harmonies of fleeting colour which the sun still lavishes upon her waters. And there is a season of the year which, with sun and mist co-operating, hangs once again her pale walls with their ancient splendour, and plays a noble part in the revival of the past. With the first days of autumn the scirocco begins to wind about the heart of her plants and creepers, and to steal into their veins. Swiftly they yield to the intoxication. Under the folds of the grey mist-mantle, they drink draught after draught of her brave wine. But another touch is needed to draw out the virtues of that liquor: after Circe, Apollo. He bends his look upon them, and they yield their stores, decking once more the walls of Venice with frescoes of scarlet, green and gold, paving once more her waterways with their old-accustomed pomp. In the Sacca della Misericordia this natural fresco has a peculiarly beautiful effect; for upon the spaces of water between the rafts that float there, the rich creepers, interwoven among the trees of the garden of the Spiriti, fling an enchanted carpet of chequered crimson and green upon a pale rose ground, covering the whole expanse, save for one space whereon is set the pale blue watermark of the sky. One may make rare studies here of the carpets and bright mats that are to be seen hung out in the pictures of the old Venetian masters. They did not copy from the East alone, or rather they copied from a greater East, whose treasures travel through a rarer element than water day after day to the shores of the western world. The complete stillness of the pools in the Sacca, undisturbed by any passing steamboat, and even unruffled by the motion of a gondola, through the protection of the intervening rafts, gives the rich pattern a durability unattainable in the waters of the canals. There is only, as it were, a faint breathing of the surface, enough to give perpetual interchange and commerce among the bold brush-strokes of colour—incessant, subtle weaving of new harmonies upon the ground-bass—the shadows deepening or relaxing, when sometimes an insect dips or a fish rises and starts a fairy circle at a touch that spreads among the colours until its delicate life is lost.

A PALACE DOOR.

And if at times we may thus see the past in the present, at other times we may dream the present back into the past. Night, the worker of so many miracles, holds a key with which we may unlock in Venice the secret of bygone times. There are hours on the lagoons when even in daylight the forgotten ages live again and we may keep company with whom we will, but in the heart of the city it is by night that we may lay hand on the pulse of her ancient life, and feel it warm to our touch, beating slow but constant behind the commotion, often the desecration, of later times. The flow of the Grand Canal is less troubled than by day: it has intervals of peace in which it may sink into the broad, dark calm of Carpaccio's waters. Palace after palace, in fearless and unstudied alternations of Byzantine, Gothic, Ogival, Renaissance, Barocco, tower above us, their pillars and balconies gleaming in faint light of moon or lamp: we seem almost to trace upon their surface the forms of men and beasts, and to clothe them once more in the gold and colour which Venice learned of her lagoons. By day we feast upon the tints still left to fall upon the waters, we praise the aged snow of crumbling stone or the shades of twisted columns, or the rich profusion of the pale Cà d'Oro. But what do we know of Venice when she shone upon the waters in true regality, a monument of all the glory that the heart or eye of man could conceive? No one has left us any detailed record of the frescoed façades of the Venetian palaces, whether on the Grand Canal or in the remoter waterways; only here and there we catch a glimpse of them on the canvases of contemporary painters. It is provokingly general among the travellers or native-lovers of Venice, who set themselves to praise her in words, to find that they have chosen a medium incapable of achieving what it was asked to do, and to throw down their weapon in the moment of trial, struck dumb by the immense wonder of their theme. They cease from their task before, it seems to us, they have well begun it, always anticipating the stinging tongue of the dragon, Incredulity. We could well forgive them their inadequacy, so frankly recognised, had they but attempted a mere catalogue of some of the frescoes on the walls. Now, it is at night alone that we can repeople them; that, as we pass along, we can look up and read into the shadowy spaces those brilliant chronicles of beauty, power and pride. It is, indeed, a heavy fate that awaits in Venice the artist who must work in words; colour and music can draw nearer, can almost attain to the reality itself; and yet by words also there is something to be conveyed of her enduring beauty. The fact which words can compass may be so told that there is born from it a sentiment of that rich atmosphere which is beyond the reach of words; they may remind or may awaken wonder, itself a new sense with which to apprehend. Even words may tell of the water snake of green and gold that writhes and gleams hour after hour in the faintly stirred depths of the canal, a creature that in the world above is a dull grey upright pole; or of golden treasures, once the refuse of the calli, transformed to splendour as they float out over the lagoon; or of the sudden lapping of the water under the wind down the north lagoon at midnight, that breaks the smooth image of the moon into a thousand ripples and passes in a wave that makes the dim lamps tremble into the narrow waterways of the city.

But it is not only the waterways of Venice that at night are eloquent of the past, that seem to take once more their ancient shape and venture near for colloquy: the streets and squares and churches are full of spirits, not unkindly, not afraid, less silent and secretive than in the busy day, when they are lonely among a people careless of them, with other thoughts, other needs and other destinies. Many a porch or gable or wide-projecting roof, or sculpture of fantastic beast or naïve saint or kneeling angel, seems to step out and call upon us in the night, catching in us perhaps as we pass by some touch of sympathy with the enduring soul of the past. One must be late indeed in Venice to secure untroubled peace. Ever and again, even after midnight, the silence of the great white campos is broken by a group scattered here and there before the door of a café; voices in eager talk will echo under a low portico, a sleepy child will clatter by in wooden pattens. But in the low-beamed, dimly lighted courts, or on the dark steps at the water-side, under some deserted sotto-portico, the sounds of the present strike across us like distant voices in a dream. The one night that lies over all the ages draws our spirit into harmony with these stones and lapping waters, that have stood through change and stress of time, that have outlived solemnity and joyous festival and have passed from gentle usage and glorious vesture into the custody of the poorest, into neglect and decay. What talk have not these courtyards overheard, what rich vesture has not swept through them, what noble thoughts and high hopes have not confided in their silence? And on the dirty steps where the children sit and play and throw their refuse into the water, what carpets have not been spread, what proud feet have not pressed to pass into the gondola and join the triumphant processional of Venice in her prime?

But what of ancient Venice? We sometimes despair of re-creating her. We ponder on Rialto, we watch her lights from the lagoons, we go in and out among her calli, peering into door and courtyard, climbing an outer stair, penetrating the recesses of sotto-portico or cellar; and many records we find of the life which once she lived, but all belong to the Venice of that second age, when she was already an established city. We cannot depopulate her and see again that company of islands gathered together in the lagoon, of various shapes and sizes, some covered with wood and undergrowth, others rising with bare backs from the water, with large and lonely outposts lying at greater distance here and there. Yet now and again come days when the spirit even of this remoter period returns to its well-nigh forgotten grave, the days when Venice lies under the rule of the rain-clouds. The inner waterways of the city lie dead like opaque marble under the dancing drops; but down the ways that lead from the lagoons the wind pours strong and restless from the sea, beating the water against the walls and into the damp vaults, a challenge from the sea to the city, from the sea unbridled and insurgent—yet not insurgent, for it has never submitted to her sway. Within Venice, along the slippery streets, there is gloom and desolation; the sun is the only visitor to whom her heart stands ever open; she would shut her gates if she could to these wild beings of cloud and wind, these houseless, grey pilgrims that, at no bidding of hers, come and claim lodging with her as they take their nomad way. I know not what of the old, wild fisher heart comes to visit Venice in these days; phantoms of old time are borne in on the gusty winds from the sea and the lagoon, and the commanding voice of the sea wind they must have known so well seems to clothe them with substantial life. Into the mist vanishes the frescoed Venice of high pomp and festival, the Venice of regal Bucintoro and banqueting of kings, of brilliant policy and stern civic control. A still deeper oblivion receives the Venice of small joys and small sorrows, of Longhi and Goldoni; and the excitement of the formless past creeps into us, when yet the future was to make—the hard life of the first dwellers upon the islands, acute and mobile in their hourly traffic with wind and sea.

ZATTERE.

There is a corner of Venice little known to the stranger, or even
to Venetians themselves, except as a passage to the cemetery
of San Michele, but not less loved on that account by those
who are happy enough to have their lot cast there. The breezes
blow with a freshness that is rare in the more confined spaces
of the city or on the Grand Canal; the tide sets into the Sacca
della Misericordia full and fresh from the northern lagoon, still
beating with the pulse of the open sea. This favoured, this
unique corner of Venice is a large square basin of water, open
on one side to the lagoon. Venice, at one time, could boast of
many such, but one by one they have been filled in with earth,
and in the sixteenth century, when the neighbouring
Fondamente Nuove were built, the Sacca della Misericordia
itself narrowly escaped inclusion in the paved parade that was
to unite the whole of North Venice from Santa Giustina to

Sant' Alvise. The fiat had gone forth, but happily it remains as yet unfulfilled, and the Sacca is still a harbour for the *zattere*, the timber rafts that are brought down from the mountains, and set here to season awhile, in sight of their old home, till at last they are borne away to do service in the works of man. A tiny hut of planks without a door is set up here and there upon the rafts, and a couple of dogs are continually upon the prowl. Something in this woodyard, the building of the rafts, the lapping of the inflowing tide against them, its waves twisted in some angle into a petulant restlessness, seems to carry us back to the primeval days before the historic settlement of the fugitives from the great mainland cities, back to the manners of the humble fishermen who lived a hard and frugal life among the low islands of the Adriatic, in constant commerce with their patron the sea, in constant vigilance against his aggression.

The night-lapping of the waves against the Sacca della Misericordia calls to mind the two toiling fishermen of Theocritus, whose life must have been strangely like that of the first dwellers on the Rivo Alto. Let us quote from Mr. Andrew Lang's translation. "Two fishers on a time together lay and slept: they had strown the dry sea-moss for a bed in their wattled cabin, and there they lay against the leafy wall. Beside them were strewn the instruments of their toilsome hands, the fishing-creels, the rods of reed, the hooks, the sails bedraggled with sea-spoil, the lines, the weels, the lobster-pots woven of rushes, the seines, two oars and an old coble upon props. Beneath their heads was a scanty matting, their clothes, their sailor's caps. Here was all their toil, here all their wealth. The threshold had never a door, nor a watch-dog: all things, all to them seemed superfluity, for Poverty was their sentinel. They had no neighbour by them, but ever against their narrow cabin gently floated up the sea." This is a page for the history of Venice in her infancy, or rather for the history of that earlier time when Venice was as yet unborn. Out among the islands of the lagoon, which on a calm, vague day of summer seem to hover in the atmosphere upon a silver haze, among those luminous paths of chrysophrase and porphyry, mother-of-pearl and opal, we shall still find some footsteps of these first Venetians unerased by tract of time.

Perhaps it is at Sant' Erasmo that the print is clearest; there are few materials that we cannot find here for reconstruction of the primeval settlement. There are the rush-roofed shelters of the boats and the rude landing-stages; there are the low, white *capane* roofed with thatch or tiles, the long, narrow, stagnant waterways, the high, grassy levels bordering the water; there are fields of reeds, and thickets or fringes of rustling poplars; there are *valli* where the fish stir and leap and gleam continuously, breaking the smooth water into a thousand ripples; there is the broad, central waterway, and countless lesser channels and pools among the reeds, where one may see a boat slowly winding, guided perhaps by children, their little figures standing out against the desolate landscape, the silence broken by no voice but theirs. Thus must Venice have been in her infancy. And if from among these lonely waterways and grassy flats of Sant' Erasmo we look forward into the future, we can anticipate the gradual evolution of a city such as Venice was afterwards to be. The building of the first mud-huts; the driving of the first close-set clumps of piles to support more solid structures; the filling of marsh-pools and strengthening of foundations; the light wooden bridges thrust across the water, as one may see them on the Lido to-day; the transition from houses of wood to houses of brick and stone, from thatch to tiles; the building of churches on the higher ground, each with its plot of grass about it; the paving of the most frequented ways, the construction of wells and chimneys, of paved campo and fondamenta; till we reach at last the city of palaces, of temples and of towers, the city of sumptuous and varied colour, the *Venezia nobilissima* of Carpaccio and Gentile Bellini.

Milton Keynes UK
Ingram Content Group UK Ltd.
UKHW042145281024
450365UK00010B/620